God With Us

Advent, Christmas, and Epiphany Sermons

by

David H. Petersen

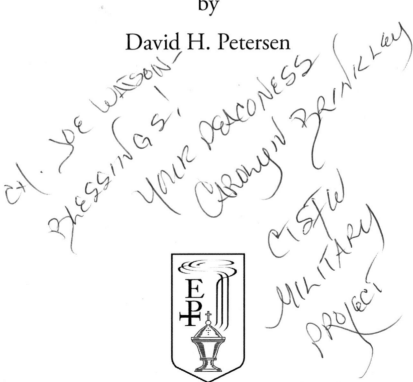

Ch. Joe Watson -
Blessings!

your Deaconess
Carolyn Brinkley

CTSFW
Military
Project

*For the saints whose Advent fast and Nativity celebrations
included early morning treks to Redeemer for the Sacrament,
where they put the first "amens" to these sermons.*

&

Table of Contents

MOVEABLE DAYS

FOREWORD

There is perhaps no other season in the church year that better embodies what we experience as Christians than the season of Advent. Observing Advent means learning to wait. It's a time of waiting and watching, a time of looking and listening. It is the season of the now, but not yet. It proclaims that the Lord is come, and yet coming still again. It tells us to look up now, for our redemption is drawing near but not yet fully here. It announces the release of the prisoners, but not yet for John the Baptist. Advent teaches us to wait.

Waiting is an art that our impatient age has forgotten. And so we are shaped by what we are unwilling to wait for. We want to harvest before the crop has fully ripened, but we are soon disappointed when what looked to be sweet fruit is, in fact, sour because of our greed and haste. We throw it away. What was full of promise now rots on the ground, discarded by unthankful hands.

This unwillingness to wait is axiomatic in our lives. But sometimes we don't cast out that which is sour. Oftentimes we live with it and become sour ourselves. Like our first parents, we reach not only for premature fruit but also fruit fully grown and yet forbidden by God. It's not that Adam and Eve were in need. They were in paradise. They had no lack for food. Likewise, it isn't for lack of things that we can't wait but rather because we have so much. We are so confident, so comfortable, and have so much that we are discontent with what God has actually given, casting it away for what He has not given. In that act of rebellion, in our greed and impatience, it is not the fruit that is sour but us.

"Everything worth having is worth waiting for," the saying goes. But for those who cannot wait, who will not wait, the blessing of waiting is lost on them because the fulfillment of promise is never theirs. Advent pulls us out of this. It teaches us to wait and to wait for the right things, for our lives are shaped by what we wait for. It forms who we are. Like the single woman waiting for a husband or the elderly man waiting, even longing, to go "home," Advent is a time to learn patience. It is a test of endurance, a time to wait. It's a time where we rehearse in the church year what we experience in our daily lives: patient endurance as we wait for the Lord to come and fulfill His promises.

The sermons in *God With Us* will help you learn to wait and to wait for the right things. You will hear not only that Christ has come in the flesh to save us from sin and death, but also that He comes still in Word and Sacrament, and that He is coming again to take us from this vale of tears to Himself. You will be reminded not just of what God in Christ has done, but what He promises to do now and in the future. You will learn to wait for Christ and the fulfillment of His promises. For if we are shaped by what we wait for, then waiting for the right things will form us and thus prepare us to receive them when they come. It will mold us into those who wait and watch for Christ: the one who came, who comes, and who is coming again.

Rev. Jason M. Braaten
Tuscola, Illinois
The Nativity of the Blessed Virgin Mary

INTRODUCTION

God's promise of a Savior gave hope to the Old Testament saints, beginning with Adam and Eve, and culminated with John the Baptist, when that prophet was given the joyful task of pointing out God in the flesh. The coming redemption of God's people is what gives every book of the Old Testament meaning, from Genesis through Malachi. Without the promise of God in the flesh, the thirty-nine books of the Old Testament are simply a quaint historical account of a delusional people. Moses, all the prophets, and the people who believed their preaching placed all of their faith in God's Word, that the woman's offspring would bruise the serpent's head. God revealed the nature of this promise through the prophets, but the clearest prophecy was preached by Isaiah to Ahaz: "Behold, the virgin shall conceive and bear a son, and shall call his name Immanuel" (Isa. 7:14). These words were remembered when the angel Gabriel appeared to Joseph, calming his fears about Mary's pregnancy and announcing that this son, Jesus, will "save his people from their sins" (Matt. 1:21), thereby fulfilling Isaiah's prophecy about Immanuel, which means "God with us."

Jesus came to crush the head of the serpent. He came to rescue His people, to buy us back from eternal death, not with gold or silver but with His holy precious blood and His innocent suffering and death. But for God to die, He must first take on flesh, be born, and live. For God to be with us, He must first become one of us. And in the fullness of time, after much anticipation (and much prophecy), Jesus was born in Bethlehem to the Virgin Mary.

The incarnation is the most spectacular thing the world has ever experienced: the true, holy, almighty, creating God put on our flesh and became man. This is a miracle beyond all miracles. From the moment of His birth, God's relationship with His people would change forever. He enfleshed Himself and became one of us in order to redeem and rescue us from sin, death, and the devil. "For we do not have a high priest who is unable to sympathize with our weaknesses, but one who in every respect has been tempted as we are, yet without sin" (Heb. 4:15).

Every year, Christians celebrate and remember this extraordinary event. We celebrate and remember, but we also look forward in anticipation to His second coming. We look forward to the fulfillment of all that He earned for us in the flesh: forgiveness of sins, life, and salvation. He lived, suffered, died, rose again, and ascended into heaven for us. Yet He is not absent from us. He very clearly told His disciples before His ascension, in the last recorded words of Matthew, that He would remain with them until the close of the age. This was an important promise. In a miracle almost as extraordinary as the incarnation, He continues to be God with us—with His Church, in the flesh—even after His ascension. After His incarnation, God would always be true God and true man simultaneously. He will never lay aside His flesh. Therefore, wherever God is present, He is present in His glorified, fleshly body. This happens in His Church, now, through the Word and the Sacraments.

His incarnation forms the substance of all Christian preaching, and it is the essence of every celebration of the Lord's Supper and Baptism, every proclamation of Absolution to repentant sinners. That's why the Christian Church gathers around preaching and the Sacraments. That's why books of sermons continue to be published and cherished in the Church. Christ is present in His body—for us, for forgiveness. The sermons in *God With Us* embody incarnational preaching. Pr. Petersen preaches an ever-present Christ, a Christ for you, a Christ with you.

ABOUT THE BOOK

In 2012 we published *Thy Kingdom Come: Lent and Easter Sermons* by David H. Petersen. Its enthusiastic reception convinced us to begin compiling another book of sermons. Lent is the great season of preparation and thus invokes a devotional character that liturgical Christians, especially Lutherans, have always cherished. The forty days of Lent culminate in the redemption event: the crucifixion, burial, and resurrection of Jesus. Advent is the church year's lesser season of preparation, but it still entreats a similar devotional response from Christians. Advent leads us to the celebration of God's birth in the flesh: His incarnation.

During these two preparatory seasons, Christians often choose to add another layer of discipline to their worship practice, such as special personal devotions or more frequent attendance at weekday services (in addition to the regular Sunday Divine Service). At Redeemer Lutheran Church, Fort Wayne, our daily Matins services yield to daily Divine Services during penitential seasons. Original sermons replace readings from the Church Fathers for our homilies, which are the sermons that you will read here in *God With Us*. Since Pr. Petersen has been preaching daily during Advent for over twelve years, some of the homiletical ideas contained in these sermons have been ruminating and maturing for years.

Redeemer follows the historic one-year series, which is almost identical to that of the Lutheran Church of the Reformation. With rare exceptions, we follow the Sunday propers of the one-year series included in *Lutheran Service Book*. In preparing sermons for *Thy Kingdom Come*, we used the daily lectionary for Lent as found in *Daily Divine Service Book: A Lutheran Daily Missal*, edited by Pr. Heath R. Curtis. However, there is no such historic daily lectionary for Advent. This necessitates some local manipulation in order to have texts from which to prepare daily sermons. Preaching texts for Advent weekdays vary. Some pastors have chosen to focus on a book of the Bible, selected pertinent topics, or Luther's Catechisms as the basis of sermons during Advent. We deliberated over how to choose a daily lectionary, using all the resources known and available to us, and in the end we crafted our own.

It is our custom at Redeemer to preach on the Gospel text for Sunday's Divine Service, and we have simply carried the theme from Sunday's propers to the rest of the week. Thus the week's Introit, Old

Testament, or Epistle text would form the basis of a weekday sermon while the Gospel reading would still be retained. Generally, these three were assigned to Monday, Tuesday, and Saturday, respectively. There does exist a lectionary for Wednesdays and Fridays of Advent in the Flurheim lectionary as provided by Zion Lutheran Church in Detroit, Michigan (available for download at www.ziondetroit.org), which we use. For our midweek service on Thursday, we chose the Lucan canticles for the first three Thursdays in Advent—the Benedictus, the Magnificat, and the Nunc Dimittis—and the Epistle text from the fourth Sunday in Advent for the final Thursday. Another break in the pattern occurs during the Third Sunday in Advent with the ember days of Wednesday, Friday, and Saturday, which have special readings and collects assigned to them as found in the aforementioned *Daily Divine Service Book*. These quarterly ember weeks correspond to the natural seasons and are a particular time of devotion, often coupled with fasting, repentance, and prayer.

While some may consider "The Twelve Days of Christmas" to be a trite and overplayed song, it actually has its roots in the liturgical year. The season of Christmas does not begin on December 1st, as commercialism would have us believe. Instead, it is properly celebrated for twelve continuous days from December 25th through the January 5th, with Epiphany the following day. Days which do not have assigned readings make use of readings from the Sundays after Christmas. Sermons for the two Sundays after Christmas have been placed in the "Moveable Days" section of the book in order to not displace any of twelve days of Christmas. The dates of the first Sunday after Christmas (Sunday within the Octave of Christmas) and the second Sunday will naturally depend on when Christmas Day falls, so please read these sermons when appropriate. The second Sunday after Christmas is not needed in years when it falls after Epiphany.

Epiphany is a flexible season that begins on January 6th, when the liturgical year calls to remembrance the appearance of the Gentile wise men who came to worship Jesus and bring Him gifts. We have included all the Sundays after Epiphany, so that they are available to you during longer Epiphany seasons. During shorter Epiphany seasons, on the Sunday before Septuagesima, it is a good liturgical practice to jump ahead to the last Sunday after Epiphany, which is always Transfiguration.

Lastly, because Thanksgiving consistently falls before St. Andrew, and because St. Andrew is always right before the first Sunday in Advent, we have placed these two sermons in the beginning of the book. However, the other saints' days, which are also date specific but may not occur in the same week every year, have been placed in the "Moveable Days" section in the back of the book. Insert these sermons into your devotional reading as appropriate. Advent flexes, waxing and waning, depending on which day of the week claims St. Andrew. Since Advent, each year, has either slightly more or fewer days, we have included enough sermons for the longest possible Advent season.

A NOTE ON BIBLE TRANSLATION AND SCRIPTURE CITATION

At Redeemer, we use the English Standard Version (ESV) for all of the readings; however, we still retain the King James Version (KJV) for our Psalmody (Introit, Gradual, and Alleluia). In the sermons, Pr. Petersen quotes mainly from the ESV, but there are times when he is preaching on the Introit or other instances that the KJV will predominate, which are thus cited. But unless otherwise marked, all other Biblical citations are from the ESV.

As we noted in *Thy Kingdom Come*, one of the distinct marks of Pr. Petersen's preaching style is the ease with which he moves between his own words and the words of Holy Scripture. He interweaves the language of the sacred text fluidly throughout each sermon. It would, therefore, be a daunting task and cumbersome in appearance to cite every Biblical reference, not to mention out of sync with the rhythm and smoothness of his preaching. Generally, Scripture references that come from the day's readings will not be specifically cited, but quotations outside of the readings will be cited. This should not cause any confusion since the day's readings are listed, which we encourage you to read first to put the sermon in its proper Biblical context.

Incarnational preaching is always bound to the Holy Scriptures, the Word of God. You cannot separate preaching from the Bible without destroying the Gospel and losing Christ. Thanks to the testimony of the Holy Spirit, we have God's sure Word from which to preach and teach. It is our pleasure to release this book of sermons, founded upon God's Word and confessing the incarnational Christ. It is our prayer that *God With Us* would aid in devotion and strengthen faith in our Lord Jesus Christ.

Rev. Michael N. Frese
Emmanuel Press
Redeemer Lutheran Church
Fort Wayne, Indiana

THANKSGIVING

Deuteronomy 8:6-18
1 Timothy 2:1-8
St. Matthew 6:25-34

In the name of the Father and of the ✠ Son and of the Holy Spirit. Amen.

Consider the dandelions, how they grow: they neither toil nor spin. They are fought with the harshest of chemicals and suffer disparaging remarks and hatred.

Our anxieties rarely come from concern over food or clothing, unless it is how that food or clothing will affect the way we look. Being fat and unattractive gets less attractive every day as our society continues its downward slip to the crassest of hedonistic materialism.

Obsessive concern about our appearance is rarely about health or the continuation of our lives. It is almost always about acceptance and desirability. The public antics of misbehaving celebrities are the face of our inward fears and desperation. Facebook and Twitter, and who knows what else, serve not just to tempt us with old girlfriends, with gossip and spying, but also to find out what we've been left out of. In the past, we could be snubbed and never know it, but now, too often, we know just how unpopular we are.

We are anxious with thoughts of how impressed the masses are with our witty remarks, how many "likes" something gets. We'll cut our best friends and family to the core if makes us popular for a fleeting moment on Facebook. And we ask, "What sort of a picture do I have to take of myself—what pose, what Photoshop magic, what pouting of the lips—to get the boys to notice me?"

Loneliness is the bane of our age. We are more desperate for approval now than ever before. We are willing to do almost anything so that someone will laugh at our jokes, will admire and respect us. The ancients would recognize this as hubris, but it is hubris so gross, so overfed and coddled, as to be beyond their imagination. Repent.

And relax. The dandelions are an example for you. They don't notice how much they are hated. They know they are loved by God. They know that He delights in their beauty as they reach up toward heaven and fulfill their destiny. They are unashamed to be dandelions, and they make no attempt to be anything else. I tell you, even Solomon in all his glory was not arrayed like one of these. But if God so clothes the grass of the field, which today is alive and tomorrow is sprayed with chemicals and thrown into the trash, will He not much more clothe you, O you of little faith? You are worth far more than dandelions. And dandelions are worth a lot.

The dandelions suffer the consequence of sin, including our warfare against them, even though they are without sin. And they do not fight back. The Lord delights in their beauty, and yet, as pious and faithful as they are, He did not take up the stuff of dandelions and redeem them.

But He has taken up your flesh. He has clothed Himself not just in your skin but also with your sin. He has declared Himself guilty for your crimes. He has gone to the cross and set Barabbas free. He has been forsaken by the Father, endured all the demands and tortures of hell and justice on your behalf, in order to draw you near. He has made Himself a sacrifice, an atonement for the life of the world, the innocent given for the guilty, in order to clothe you with His grace.

So do not ask, "What shall we eat?" for the Lord has said, "Take, eat, this is My body." Do not ask, "What shall we drink?" for the Lord has said, "Drink of it, the cup of the New Testament in My blood, all of you." And do not ask, "What shall we wear? Do I look fat? How can I get the world to notice me, to care about me?" for the Lord has covered your nakedness and shame with His righteousness and honor. You are beautiful to Him, worth all He had, worth the life of the Son.

If you are lonely, if you think yourself unattractive, boring, or dumb, read the Song of Songs. It is a love poem from God to you. Hear there the Lord's borderline-erotic attraction for you, His thumping desire, His eager love. For you are worth more than the birds of the air, the lilies of the field, or even the holy angels. You are worth more than your family or friends or co-workers could ever imagine, even more than you yourself wish you were worth.

Now that is something to be thankful for.

In ✠ Jesus' name. Amen.

St. Andrew, Apostle

November 30

Ezekiel 3:16-21
Romans 10:8-18
St. John 1:35-42

In the name of the Father and of the ✠ Son and of the Holy Spirit. Amen.

The piety of the Church shifts over time. All Saints' Day is more popular than it used to be. It overshadows Reformation in a way that would surely surprise our fathers. St. Paul will probably always be the favorite saint of Lutheranism, but there is an increased interest in Sts. Nicholas, Patrick, and a handful of others. St. Andrew, however, even though he is one of the twelve, never seems to be popular among us.

He was a fisherman, which is why they like him in Malta, and the brother of St. Peter, which is why they like him in Scotland. He was also something of a missionary, bringing Peter to Christ and bringing the Greeks to Christ. In our evangelism-obsessed age, you'd think that would make him a favorite. I don't know why it hasn't.

Perhaps Andrew is too associated with Advent to be popular. His day begins the church year. And there is something in Advent, something austere and serious, something of John the Baptist, Andrew's first rabbi, that sends our fallen flesh running away.

St. John stands on the Jordan's banks. He is stuck in the desert like Moses, stuck in camel's hair with locusts in his teeth, stuck in a fiery cry: "Repent. The ax is laid at the root." No one escapes his harsh preaching. From that grim and barren place, he sees the promised one in the promised land and prophesies, "Behold the Lamb of God! The Law in Him is fulfilled." And no one is left out.

4

However stuck John may be, his disciples are not stuck. They move. They follow the Lamb. The Lamb turns and speaks, "What do you seek?" And they ask in response, "Where are you staying?"

That is significant. They are seeking someplace to stay. John is stuck in the desert. There is no future there. Where does the Lamb stay? How does one live in this world? That is what our fallen flesh is always asking. We are always seeking *technia* rather than *sophia*. We want little bits of practical wisdom, ways to get ahead, a place to stay in this world.

"Come and see," says the Lamb. Little do they know that He is inviting them to come and die. One doesn't live except he die. The Lamb does not abide in this short life. He has no practicality. He has made no provision to feed Himself or to find a safe place to sleep. There is nowhere for Him to lay His head but on the cross. He has come to be a sacrifice. If John is stuck in the desert, Jesus is stuck in His Father's obedience.

But John never promised them a soft life anyway. The Lamb comes to take away sin, not to bestow feather beds. John told them that Jesus is the Lamb of God. That can only mean that He is the Passover Lamb, the one who is slaughtered to shield His people from the angel of death by His blood.

Sadly, such is the persistence of fallen men that we can be told *lamb* but hear *lion*. They sought, no doubt, the wrong thing. But it did not matter because, in truth, He sought them.

Here is Advent and Andrew's proclamation: "You don't go to God. He comes to you." He seeks. He saves. That is the point of John's question from prison: "Are you the coming one?" Because that is what we desperately need, not a place to stay but a God who comes to us.

Hearing John, they followed Jesus. By grace, they stayed with the Lamb. They stayed even unto their own martyrdoms, even if Andrew never gets much honor of his own. But such is the way of the Advent disciples of John. Such is the way of the kingdom: its honor belongs to Christ, even as does its righteousness, but both—the kingdom of Christ and His righteousness—are declared to belong to the saints.

What Andrew gets, you get as well.

Behold, the Lamb of God, the coming one, who has come into the world.

In ✠ Jesus' name. Amen.

The First Sunday in Advent

Jeremiah 23:5-8
Romans 13:8-14
St. Matthew 21:1-9

In the name of the Father and of the ✠ Son and of the Holy Spirit. Amen.

Zechariah's line is the essence of Christianity: "Your king is coming to you."

Advent, of course, means *coming*. We often speak of the threefold coming of Christ. He came in flesh, in a body, born of the Virgin to be a sacrifice for sins. He will come again, in flesh, in a body, on the last day to judge the living and the dead. And He comes now, in flesh, in a body, in the Holy Communion.

The Lord who comes in His risen body in the Holy Communion also comes in His Word. He is present in the preaching of His Church and in the Bible. He also comes with His Holy Spirit in the name of the Father at Holy Baptism, where He makes sinners into His temple. He comes in the Absolution. He is present in holy marriage as well, in the bond of fellowship, and in the hearts of His people.

This is nothing new. Zechariah said, "Your king is coming to you." The Lord was present with His people before the incarnation. He was the rock that watered them, the pillar that led them. He was in the holy of holies, sitting on the mercy seat, shielding them from the Law's accusations and their sins, accepting their praise and hearing their prayers. He is the Lord who walked in the garden and spoke from the bush.

But once the Lord came in flesh, once He took up our cause in the Virgin's womb, He became meek, almost embarrassingly so. When resistance to His ministry mounted, He withdrew. Five times in Matthew's Gospel, the Lord runs away. When Joseph heard what

Herod planned, the Lord fled, out of Bethlehem to Egypt. When He heard that John had been arrested, He fled to Galilee. When He heard that the Pharisees were conspiring to kill Him, He fled. When He heard that John had been killed, He fled into the desert. And after the Pharisees again challenged Him in Gennesaret, He fled to the region of Tyre and Sidon. Finally, when they come to get Him in the garden, He submits like a sheep to the slaughter.

But there on Palm Sunday, He comes, humble, riding on a donkey, and yet, at the same time, forceful. He will not be stopped. He tells them what is to happen. The disciples go and get the donkey. Without anyone telling them what to do, the people spontaneously pave His road with their clothes and branches. They shout, "Hosanna to the Son of David!" They know that He is the king even though they really don't know quite what that means.

But they do know something is up and something is not right. Even as they offer Him tribute and praise, they shake in fear. He is humble, but there is power in Him, power that is being stirred up against the devil, to rescue us. He is coming. But we, like they, are not so sure we want to be rescued. We don't like the old boss, but Jesus can be a bit bossy Himself. How can we stand in His presence and not be destroyed? How can we stand in His presence and keep our selfish ways? A proverb of men reads, "Better the devil known than unknown."

We are right to be afraid. The Lord withdrew during His ministry, not because He was weak or cowardly but because He is the high priest and the king. No one takes His life from Him. He lays it down of His own accord, at the proper time and in the proper way. He rides toward His throne, His glory, and His power. He rides to the cross. It is terrible to behold, worse than the rushing wind that Elijah felt at his back as he hid in the crack of the mountain. The Lord does not take His kingdom by force, by violence, but it is most certainly violent. He suffers it. He endures violence to win His kingdom back. He pays for it with His own blood. And there is no going back.

Hosanna means *save us* in Hebrew. That is what the people are shouting as He rides. They are asking Him to go and die, whether they know it or not, asking Him to save them. He is riding not only whether they know it or not but also whether they ask for it or not. They may not want to be rescued. They might be terrified of what this costs, of what this will mean, but His Father wants them rescued and He fulfills His Father's will. He is the Lord who will not leave things alone. He is the Lord who comes, and He will not be stopped simply because they, and we, are not worthy or smart enough. He comes to seek and to save.

Repent, the king draws near. Rejoice, your king is coming to you. He will not leave you alone or pretend as though everything is okay. He is the king who comes.

So He comes to earth, not in a burning bush or a pillar of fire but through a virgin—a weak and crying baby in need of His mother's love. He comes, in weakness and humility, to be nailed to the cross and left there to die. He comes, though, weak as He might be, with power unlike any other. He is purposeful and certain. He knows what He is doing. And so it is that He also comes alive out of death.

And then the really great surprise: He comes out of death to the fearful, failure disciples, and He is not mad. He holds no grudge. The violence is over, all done to Him in their stead. So He comes gentle and kind, reconciling and peaceful. "Peace be with you," He says.

Zechariah had it quite right: "Your king is coming to you." And what a king He is! You do not go to Him. You do not know the way and you do not have the strength. He comes to you. He seeks. He saves. He does what you could never do. He makes you His own. Soon He will come again, not humble, not riding on a donkey, not hidden in bread and wine, not fleeing to the mountains, but in glory. Hosanna, Son of David! Hosanna! Come, Lord Jesus! Come quickly!

In ☩ Jesus' name. Amen.

Monday of Advent i

Psalm 25

In the name of the Father and of the ✠ Son and of the Holy Spirit. Amen.

The word Advent is derived from a Latin word that means *coming*. Advent is a short season focused on the second coming of the Messiah, but it culminates in the celebration of His first coming in the flesh in Bethlehem. Because Advent culminates with Christmas, Christians are sometimes confused by the seasonal emphasis on the end times. But it is really quite simple. Jesus isn't about to be born, and, yet, He is most certainly about to return. We see in His birth a foreshadowing not only of the cross and resurrection but also of the end. The bridegroom is coming.

If He is coming, then we are waiting. God's people have always been waiting.

> Wait for the LORD; be strong, and let your heart take courage; wait for the LORD! (Ps. 27:14)

> [T]hey who wait for the LORD shall renew their strength; they shall mount up with wings like eagles; they shall run and not be weary; they shall walk and not faint. (Isa. 40:31)

From the time of Adam until John, the people waited for the fulfillment of the temple to arrive, for God to take up their cause in His body and to sacrifice Himself in their stead. They were waiting for the Messiah to be born and to die. David, despite his many sins, was confident: no one who waits on the Lord shall be put to shame. David waited for the incarnation, for the crucifixion, for the lifting of the Law and the forgiveness of sins to be won. Those years, from the birth of

Christ to His resurrection, are the pinnacle of history, the culmination of time. It was what the world waited for.

That waiting is now done, but we are still waiting. We wait for the same Lord. We wait for His return. He says, "Behold, I am coming soon, bringing my recompense with me, to repay each one for what he has done. I am the Alpha and the Omega, the first and the last, the beginning and the end" (Rev. 22:12-13).

We want that recompense. We want it because Christ has paid for us, and it is therefore unjust that we should still suffer in our sins and bear the burden of our shame. He has paid in full and we are free. And yet, while we wait, while we endure, we suffer from our sins and the sins of others. So we are eager for the end, for the recompense and reward, for the integrity and uprightness of the Christ, our Lord, our Savior. We are eager for that which has been bought for us to be fully given to us, for the good work begun in us to be complete. We wait with no less eagerness than our forefathers who waited for the Messiah's birth.

And that is why it is so easy to pray with David: "Lead me in thy truth, and teach me: for thou *art* the God of my salvation; on thee do I wait all the day" (Ps. 25:5 KJV, emphasis added). Thanks be to God. The bridegroom is coming.

In ✠ *Jesus' name. Amen.*

TUESDAY OF ADVENT I

Jeremiah 23:5-8

In the name of the Father and of the ✠ Son and of the Holy Spirit. Amen.

This prophecy from Jeremiah, that the Lord shall no longer be the one who brought the people out of Egypt but shall now be the Lord our righteousness, is no small thing. The chief event of the history of Israel was the Exodus. It wasn't the only event, but it was the chief and the defining event. The prophets recognized the creation and the call of Abraham. They knew of Noah and his deliverance from the Flood. But the great event—that which gave birth to them as a nation and made them God's people—was the slaughter of the Passover lamb that spared them from the angel of death, the passage through the birth canal of the Red Sea on dry ground that delivered them from enslavement, and the leading of the pillar that led to the giving of the Law on Sinai.

That was it. So to change God's self-description from "the Lord who brought us out of the land of Egypt" to "the Lord is our righteousness" indicates that the Exodus wasn't the chief event anymore. It was only a foreshowing of what God would do. It was a type, not the fulfillment, and greater things were coming.

We live in those days of greater things. Judah is saved. Israel dwells securely. The kingdom has been reunited and restored. The throne is returned to David. The priest in the order of Melchizedek, the king of righteousness, has offered Himself as a sacrifice. He is the Lamb and the Pillar and the Law. And He is more: He is our righteousness. Therefore we no longer say, "He is the Lord who brought us out of Egypt," but we say, "As the Lord lives He has brought us from the ends of the earth. He has gathered us by His death on the cross and made us His people by declaring us righteous."

The central event in the history of the universe is the sacrifice of the Son to reconcile humanity back to the Father. All His other acts, every fiber of goodness in creation, echo or foreshow or deliver this. Thus St. Paul simply says, "We preach Christ crucified."

In ☩ Jesus' name. Amen.

WEDNESDAY OF ADVENT I

James 5:7-11
St. Luke 4:14-22

In the name of the Father and of the ✠ Son and of the Holy Spirit. Amen.

The Nazarene, the branch that shoots up out of David's stump, returns to Nazareth. There He proclaims the year of the Lord's favor. Now is the hour of salvation. Today the Scriptures are fulfilled. The kingdom of God is at hand.

But even in their amazement, some in Nazareth mock the Lord. "Isn't this Joseph's son?" is to ask not merely "Isn't this an ordinary man, like us," but also "Isn't this the child of Joseph's lust, conceived before marriage?" We are a sophisticated and worldly people. We know what causes a baby to be born a mere six months after the wedding. It is not that we mind. It is that they want to pretend they are holy, and we know they are not, and we will not allow them to think they are better than us. Joseph and his family are just as bad as us, or worse. How dare they pretend to be better? Who is this Jesus, the son of Joseph, to put on airs and claim to be the anointed one, to pretend His mother is a virgin?

Why do we worry so much about other people's bragging? So what if their stories are inaccurate? Why does it bother us if someone gets praise we don't think he deserves? We're not hurt by it. If pride is a terrible sin, it must be worse to be proud of not being proud like others. If it is a sin to be a hypocrite, it must be worse to look down on hypocrites and feel superior in our pretend humility and honesty.

It is easy for us to let Jesus be who He claims to be, the son of a virgin, because we are not from Nazareth. It is harder to take our brothers-in-law or co-workers. But if you do not love your neighbor, you do not love God. "Do not grumble against one another, brothers, so that you may not be judged; behold, the Judge is standing at the door" (Jas. 5:9). Repent.

The year of the Lord's favor is not the year of the Lord's tyranny. He will not force Himself on anyone in Nazareth or anywhere in the world. If the people of Nazareth will not have Him, if they choose instead to go their own way—to insist that their sins don't matter or that they aren't as bad as those self-righteous types from Jerusalem; to remain in captivity, blindness, and oppression—then He will allow them. They get the god they want. The favor of the Lord is a gift. It is the essence of a gift in that it is not a burden or requirement and can be rejected.

But whether they want it or not, whether they believe it or not, the Lord's favor is there in the Son—not of Joseph, but of Mary. The favor announced to Mary by the angel Gabriel is extended to all humanity through her Son. He can't be stopped. He seeks not their approval, but their salvation. He will buy them back out of death. He will pay the price even for those who will never benefit from it. He is like a father who pays child support for children who hate him, but he does it without regret or anger.

There is nothing forcing the mockers in Nazareth to stay in captivity. The gates of hell are broken. He goes in and seeks them out. He beseeches them to depart from the prison, to walk out the open gates. He weeps over their unnecessary sorrow. But He is not a tyrant. His gifts may be refused and lie wasted on the floors of hell.

And what of us? In a very real sense, our Lord is Joseph's son. He adopts Joseph even as Joseph adopts Him. The Lord is unashamed to be called his son, not because Joseph was innocent of what the gossipers in Nazareth snickered about (though he was), but because Joseph was redeemed by grace through faith, and the Lord came to make families whole and to give a place to the outcasts and hurting and ashamed. He is the Lord of adoption, and adoption does not make second-class families but real families. Every Christian is adopted by Joseph and calls Jesus *brother*. If the Lord came for those who are too proud to accept His gifts, He certainly came for those who are broken and desperate for the same, and He certainly welcomes them to His family.

The Nazarene, the branch that shoots up out of David's stump, thus returns to Nazareth, but He is on His way to Calvary. He proclaims the year of the Lord's favor, for now is the hour of salvation. Today the Scriptures are fulfilled. The kingdom of God is at hand. There is hope for His people. There is hope for those who suffer unkind gossip, whether it is true or not—which is to say, there is hope for us—and there is a family, a father, a brother, a bridegroom for us.

In ✠ Jesus' name. Amen.

Thursday of Advent 1

St. Luke 1:46-55

In the name of the Father and of the ✠ Son and of the Holy Spirit. Amen.

St. Mary responds to St. Elizabeth's greeting and John's natal leaping with a hymn echoing several songs from the Old Testament. The hymn has two parts. The first is St. Mary's praise as a direct response to what God, her Savior, has done to her (verses 46-49). She magnifies and rejoices in the God who is her Savior. The second part is a description of the merciful Messianic reversals which have always been known by God's people (verses 50-55). He scatters the proud, puts down the mighty, and sends the rich away empty while exalting the lowly, filling the hungry, and speaking mercifully and kindly to weak and disenfranchised people.

The whole hymn hinges on verse 48. There Mary gives the cause of her rejoicing. She rejoices because God, her Savior, has regarded her.

When it comes to pass that God turns His face toward us, contrary to what we might expect because of our sins, there is nothing but grace and salvation. The Lord looks upon us with compassion. This is how He regarded Abel and his offering, but He did not regard Cain. We see much of this also in the Psalter where we learn to pray that God would lift up His countenance upon us, that He would not hide His countenance from us, that He would make His face shine upon us, and so forth. So, too, this is precisely what God promises to do in the Aaronic benediction: He promises to lift up His countenance upon us, that is, to regard us.

This is the source of St. Mary's rejoicing. She has been regarded by God, her Savior. She has found undeserved favor in His sight. She stands in a long line of reversals, of lowly people being exalted and of old barren women conceiving children.

In a sense, of course, the mercy and grace of God in Christ is always unexpected, and yet it should be expected by the baptized. Mercy, grace, and forgiveness are the constant character of the God of Abraham. The baby placed into St. Mary's womb by the overshadowing of the Holy Spirit is not a surprise; it is the obvious and necessary culmination of history. It is the fulfillment of God's Word and promise. It is the necessary action for the God who gave dominion to Adam and Eve and who refused to let Satan steal them away. The very fact that Adam and Eve weren't immediately destroyed upon eating the forbidden fruit— that God came seeking them in the garden, like unto the fact that our world has not yet been destroyed—is a sure sign of God's mercy. He did not turn His face away from them even though they had turned their faces away from Him. He sought them out, and He turned their faces back toward Himself with a promise.

Mary herself regards this as the chief thing. She says, "Behold, since He has regarded me, all generations will call me blessed."† Indeed, all generations do call her blessed, but not her alone. For the Lord has never stopped regarding you, counting your hairs, working out your salvation. He keeps His promise. Mary's Son has made atonement, has reconciled the world to His Father, has sacrificed Himself to draw all men unto Himself that they would regard Him as He regards them. This is the countenance of God in the baby born of Mary.

In ✠ Jesus' name. Amen.

---

† For more on this verse as the key to the Magnificat and for some of the language in this sermon, see Martin Luther, "The Sermon on the Mount and the Magnificat," in *Luther's Works*, American Edition (55 vols.; ed. Jaroslav Pelikan and Helmut T. Lehmann; Philadelphia: Muehlenberg and Fortress, and St. Louis: Concordia, 1955-86), 21:321.

Friday of Advent i

Titus 2:1-10
St. Matthew 21:28-32

In the name of the Father and of the ✠ Son and of the Holy Spirit. Amen.

The parable of the two sons was told in the temple in Jerusalem early in the week before our Lord laid down His life for the life of the world. He had not yet instituted the Supper or been fully betrayed by Judas, but He had already ridden to the hosannas, and His remaining days could be counted on one hand even if you were missing a few fingers. There in the temple the Pharisees had feigned indignation. They were seeking to trap Him and asked, "By what authority are you doing these things?"

Rather than answer that the Spirit of the Lord was upon Him, that He had been anointed for these things, that He was teaching in His temple and not their temple, He exposed their duplicity. They would not answer a question about John, whether he was from God or not, because they did not actually care about the truth or legitimate authority. They only cared about how they were perceived by the crowds.

Immediately following this, He asks them, "What do you think? A man had two sons. He asked them to work in his vineyard. One said he would but didn't. He was a liar. He secretly hated his father. The other said no. He was a rebel, but then he had a change of heart and did what his father asked. Who did the will of his father?"

The prod in this parable is the Lord's question, "What do you think?" It is an invitation to stop thinking about what the people think and to start thinking about what God thinks. The tax collectors and prostitutes were entering the kingdom of God even though they were sinners. They had a change of heart. They repented. Even though they were sinners, eventually they did the will of the Father. And if there was room for them, if it was not too late for them—even as late as Monday or Tuesday in Holy Week, even while they were intent on killing Him—it was then not too late for the Pharisees. The parable of the two sons is a parable of compassion. The Lord was reaching out to the Pharisees, extending an invitation, one more time.

As you know, we tend to be more like the Pharisees than the tax collectors. We are outwardly pious, but we are skeptical of the supernatural. We want to believe John's fiery message, but it is hard for us to believe that it is real. We harbor secret doubts and secret sins. We calculate the cost of what we say at work, on Facebook, at family gatherings. We look around to see who is listening, and we care very little that God is listening. Repent. Stop thinking about what people think of you and start thinking about what God thinks.

John the Baptist's message is also for us. The axe is already laid to the root. Now is the day of salvation. Tomorrow may never come. But the Lamb of God is here. He is the sacrifice who stands in our stead, who shields us from the angel of death, whose blood forgives and spares us. Our Father calls us to work in the vineyard as He calls us to rest on the Sabbath. The vineyard is not a vineyard of toil. It is a garden plump with the harvest. And the harvest is not grapes; it is wine. The purpose of the vineyard is to make glad the hearts of men.

These are the only two things John preaches: "Repent, for the kingdom of God is at hand" and "Behold the Lamb of God who takes away the sin of the world." In these two statements are all of the prophets and the only true preparation for either Christmas or the end.

So what do you think? A man had two sons ...

In ✠ Jesus' name. Amen.

SATURDAY OF ADVENT I

Romans 13:8-14

In the name of the Father and of the ✠ Son and of the Holy Spirit. Amen.

St. Paul admonishes us to owe no one anything, but to love each other. This is like people saying they only want to be happy. Really? Just that? Just happy, nothing else? Of course not, because happy is everything. Only the most self-absorbed (and we've all been there) can say, "I just want to be happy," as though he were asking for a small thing.

When St. Paul says to owe no one anything except love, he is saying that we should owe one another everything. Love fulfills the Law. All the commandments, those terrors of our conscience, are assumed into this: Love one another. And if we might have pretended that we were innocent of adultery, murder, and theft—which would be to ignore the Lord's clear teaching in the Sermon on the Mount—this law leaves no doubt that we've failed completely. Love does no wrong. Love is perfect. "Love your neighbor as yourself" might as well be written in blood, in letters three feet high, translated as "Go to hell because you're a sinner."

That is the Law's accusing. But St. Paul doesn't seem to be in an accusing mood here. He is not trying to strip our souls bare of all works and lead us to the anxious bench. He is simply instructing us in the way of righteousness. Christ has fulfilled the Law for us. He has loved us as Himself. He rode into Jerusalem, even as He was born in Bethlehem, in order to lay down His life, holding nothing back from us. Thus our salvation is nearer now than when we first believed.

So let us live in Him, forgiven and loved. Let us forgive one another. Being loved by God in Christ, let us love one another, casting off the works of darkness, putting on the armor of light.

And how might we do that? How might we keep the Law and love one another without fail, without holding back? Setting our will to do it or making promises and resolutions has never worked before, and it won't work now. How might we keep the Law which we've never yet kept before? By putting on the Lord Jesus Christ. That is it. It is the only way. It is in being loved, being forgiven, being fed the Holy Supper that not only is sin forgiven but faith is also strengthened. In that—those things that God has given for His Church, for her faith and life—the Holy Spirit takes up residence and works do follow. The only way for sinners like us to keep the Law is to have the Law kept for us.

St. Paul's admonition can only be spoken to Christians because only those who trust that they are loved by Christ are free to love one another.

Still, no matter what sort of mood Paul is in or how nice we mean it, the Law always accuses. It describes the works and life of Christ in us, to be sure. He loves us, and through us He loves our neighbors. That is true. But if we look too closely, what do we see? We see that we have interfered, that the desires of our flesh have gotten in the way, that we have sinned and fallen short, that we are sinners who deserve to be damned because we have not loved our neighbors as ourselves but have haughtily judged them as unworthy of our love.

So repent again. Cast off the works of darkness. Be covered anew with Him who kept and fulfilled the Law for you.

This is the constant cycle and life of the Christian whether it is Advent or Christmas, Lent or Easter, a wedding or a funeral. Repent and rejoice and repeat. Love your neighbor and fail and be loved by Christ and then love your neighbor and fail and be loved by Christ and again and again and again. The only hope for us, the only way we will be saved, is if Christ Himself has kept the Law for us and puts Himself on us. Thanks be to God, that is exactly what He has done in His death and resurrection, and He has bestowed it upon us in Holy Baptism. To put on the Lord Jesus Christ is to be baptized and to commune and to be absolved.

In ✠ *Jesus' name. Amen.*

The Second Sunday in Advent

Malachi 4:1-16
Romans 15:4-13
St. Luke 21:25-36

In the name of the Father and of the ✠ *Son and of the Holy Spirit. Amen.*

The day of the Lord's return will set the wicked and the proud ablaze in hell's tortuous fire. They will suffer terribly and know great terror, for during this life they lived as if they were the only ones who mattered. They loved their families and they loved Christmas. They loved Jimmy Stewart and teared up at "God Bless America." They just didn't love Jesus, not the real Jesus, not the one who came to suffer and die, the one who said, "Take up your cross and follow Me," and "No one comes to the Father but by Me." They will see the signs, too late, in sun, moon, stars, earth, and sea. They will see them as a gathering of armies on the border, as imminent and painful death, as the end of all good things. It will be for them impending and total doom.

Repent. This is what justice requires of us. We are the wicked. What was written in former days has been written for our instruction, and yet we do not live in harmony and hope. We live for ourselves. We think it is admirable that we love our families and those who love us, but in this we are no different than the Gentiles. Loving Christmas and eggnog and feasting, loving presents and gaudy decorations and Rudolph does not make one a Christian. Repent. If we were judged by our lives, by our works, by what we loved, we would be destroyed as stubble in a fire.

The terrible day is coming, but for us who have joy now in Christ, the day will be pure joy. Our Lord directs our attention to what's going on in the world now. In politics and climate change, in violent crime and loss of rights, in news of wars and reminders that sometimes the sky rains down bombs on young soldiers and sailors relaxing on a quiet Sunday morning in Hawaii, we see signs of the end. In disasters, economic upheaval, and the simple sorrow of being the target of gossip, we see that this world cannot endure. But Jesus doesn't want to turn us into Chicken Littles, scrambling about in a panic. He wants us to lift our heads and hearts in glad anticipation. Our redemption, our Jesus, is drawing near. Rejoice!†

Look to those signs in sun, moon, and stars, in earth, sea, and even in your own life. Look to the cross, to war, to death, and see beautiful blossoms, doves, and rainbows. They point you to God's grace and promises. They are ushering in peace and tranquility, the end of war. Your enemies will be no more. Sin will lose all appeal. Temptation will have no power. There will be no one to either accuse or hurt you. The good work begun in you will be complete. Your justification and your sanctification will match perfectly. Creation itself will rejoice to see you revealed as a son of God. And you will rejoice. You will be glad, for the kingdom of God will come to you and never be taken away.

Now, however, you suffer. You know many hardships, most of them secret and internal. You endure in prayer and faith, by Word and Sacrament, waiting for the day of revelation, for the apocalyptic culmination of your hope. For then, at last, the wrath of God will pass over you, for you are marked with the blood of the Lamb. The Lord Himself is with you, is on your side. He loves you. And He is coming back to get you.

This is not the end we deserve, but it is the end that He has promised, the end that He has won for us.

The only way, however, for there to be joy in heaven and on earth at the coming of the Lord Jesus Christ in His glory and judgment is if there is joy now. The Lord, who came by the Virgin to lay down His life as a sacrifice for the sins of all the world and to take it up again as

---

† This paragraph is modified from a Facebook status quote by Rev. Rick Sawyer, 12/8/2013.

a renunciation of hell and death, now comes in His Holy Word and Sacrament so that—even now, while yet in this flesh and yet afflicted with the old Adam; even now, while you slog through this valley of sorrow—you might have joy.

And if the Lord comes now and makes you His temple; if He visits you in this painful, sad, and broken world despite your sins and does not look away from your nakedness and shame but comes to cover and protect you; if He declares you righteous and holy now, then there is nothing to fear, and much in which to rejoice, on the last day. For if He comes now in grace and mercy according to His Word, He will come then in the same way on the last day—in grace and mercy—only then it will be visible and with power, and it will finish what was begun in you at your baptism. And then it will not abide alongside of sorrow but will fully and finally banish it forever.

Thus the fig tree is in bloom. Summer is near. The smell of blossoms fills the air. Fruit to eat and wine to drink will soon be here as well. You know what fig buds mean. It means summer is coming. So look here and see the fig buds of Jesus' body and blood, His inspired Word, His Absolution, Holy Baptism. He visits you now. He comes to you in your hour of need, *now*, in grace and mercy, the crucified and risen Lord, for your sake and for your good. The world is evil. You are surrounded by danger, by temptation, by constant injustice, but Jesus is faithful. Jesus is faithful! He has ascended, but He has not abandoned you. He comes to visit you, *now*, with mercy in His wings, with a promise and hope, with comfort. His current coming in Word and Sacrament shows that summer is coming, that winter will end, that He has not forgotten you. He is the fig leaf that foreshows the end. His body and blood are the foretaste of the feast to come. He covers your nakedness and shame. You are redeemed, washed clean in the blood of the Lamb, ready for the end. Straighten up. Lift up your head. Rejoice. The Lord comes in grace and mercy.

In ✠ Jesus' name. Amen.

Monday of Advent 2

Psalm 80

In the name of the Father and of the ✠ Son and of the Holy Spirit. Amen.

The collect hints at a problem. It asks the Lord to make us ready so that by His coming we are able to serve Him with pure minds. If the Lord does not make us ready, then His coming will be in terror. We will not serve Him with pure minds but instead will be cast into eternal fire.

The Lord stirs up our hearts and prepares us for His coming on the last day by His Word.

We sing in the Antiphon from Isaiah: "Say ye to the daughter of Zion, Behold, thy salvation cometh; And the Lord shall cause his glorious voice to be heard; Ye shall have gladness of heart."†

The voice of the Lord is heard, that is, His Word is heard. And the daughter—those who hear it as the Word of their own Father—has gladness of heart. This is because the daughter hears the voice not of judgment, but of welcome. The world does not hear it. The world only sees the terrible signs in sun, moon, and sea. Without the Word of the Father welcoming and rescuing us, there is only terror.

Thus the Lord, in His mercy, prepares us for life and for death and for the end of the world with His Word. His Word causes a change in us. It moves us from hostility and fear to joy, from sin to holiness. Thus we sing in the Introit from Psalm 80: "Turn us again, O God, and cause thy face to shine; and we shall be saved." We could translate that literally as "Repent us again, O God." We are asking God to turn us away from ourselves and toward Him. We are asking that He cast the works of darkness off of us and cause us to mourn over our sins. We

---

† Isa. 62:11b; 30:30, 29 KJV

27

want Him to preach the Law, the truth, to us and then to preach also His good news and welcome to us. For if He regards us, as He regarded His handmaiden Mary, we shall be saved.

That same word *turn*, or *repent*, is used again in the Introit. We pray: "Return, we beseech thee, O God of hosts: look down from heaven, and behold, and visit this vine." We are asking God to repent, to turn away from His wrath and to turn His face toward us in mercy. Again, we are asking that He regard us, that He look down from heaven with favor, as He has regarded Mary, in mercy and grace.

Finally, the Introit beseeches God to send the Messiah lest everything else be in vain: "Let thy hand be upon the man of thy right hand, upon the son of man whom thou madest strong for thyself."

The Messiah is made strong for the Lord in order to fulfill His will, to turn the heart of the Father to His children and save us. Thus in Him can we be, and are we, regarded from heaven with favor. The Messiah is stronger than sin, death, or hell. He is stronger than Satan, and He is stronger than our pride.

The Introit doesn't quote the whole Psalm. Right after the verse that prays for the Messiah to be made strong, the Psalm prays: "So will not we go back from thee: quicken us, and we will call upon thy name."

And one more time it repeats the verse from earlier: "Turn us again, O Lord God of hosts, cause thy face to shine; and we shall be saved."

That is how the Lord stirs up our hearts and prepares us for His coming on the last day. His Word reveals that He is favorably inclined toward us through the Messiah and that He comes in mercy. Thus are we spared hell's fire and terror on the last day and enabled to serve Him with pure minds.

In ✠ Jesus' name. Amen.

Tuesday of Advent 2

Malachi 4:1-16

In the name of the Father and of the ✠ Son and of the Holy Spirit. Amen.

When the prophet Malachi describes the day of wrath like a burning oven, he is drawing upon the work of earlier prophets:

> You will make them as a blazing oven when you appear. The LORD will swallow them up in his wrath, and fire will consume them. (Ps. 21:9)

> They are all adulterers; they are like a heated oven whose baker ceases to stir the fire, from the kneading of the dough until it is leavened. (Hos. 7:4)

> For with hearts like an oven they approach their intrigue; all night their anger smolders; in the morning it blazes like a flaming fire. All of them are hot as an oven, and they devour their rulers. All their kings have fallen, and none of them calls upon me. (Hos. 7:6-7)

> For behold, the day is coming, burning like an oven, when all the arrogant and all evildoers will be stubble. The day that is coming shall set them ablaze, says the LORD of hosts, so that it will leave them neither root nor branch. (Mal. 4:1)

This picture of God's wrath also lines up with the New Testament word we usually translate as *hell*. In Greek, it is *Gehenna*. That is the Greek name of the valley of Hinno, a narrow valley south of Jerusalem where children were sacrificed to pagan gods by fire. After Malachi, the term Gehenna is the word generally used to denote hell, the place of final punishment by fire of the reprobate.

Twice in Matthew's Gospel, our Lord directly connects Gehenna (or hell) and fire.† He does so in Matthew 5: "But I say to you that everyone who is angry with his brother will be liable to judgment; whoever insults his brother will be liable to the council; and whoever says, 'You fool!' will be liable to the hell of fire" (v. 22). That is Gehenna of fire. He does it again in Matthew 6: "But if God so clothes the grass of the field, which today is alive and tomorrow is thrown into the oven, will he not much more clothe you, O you of little faith?" (v. 30).

But Malachi has more to say than what the end will be for unbelievers. He continues:

> But for you who fear my name, the sun of righteousness shall rise with healing in its wings. You shall go out leaping like calves from the stall. And you shall tread down the wicked, for they will be ashes under the soles of your feet, on the day when I act, says the Lord of hosts. (Mal. 4:2-3)

The oven is only for those who do not fear His name. For those who fear His name, the fire is not a destroying oven, but the warming and life-giving sun. Malachi gives one of the most delightful pictures of joy in the Old Testament: "You shall go out leaping like calves from the stall." We would probably say, "You will frolic like puppies or kittens." What he means is that you will lose all self-awareness and fear of being laughed at, of embarrassing yourself. You will dance like no one is watching and cease to care whether you look a fool. You will be overcome and surprised by joy, free at last to be as the Lord intended, free to be loved and not judged, free to bask in the forgiveness and acceptance of the Lord.

Thus the day of wrath is also "the great and awesome day of the Lord." It is the day when St. John's proclamation turns the hearts of

---

† Allen C. Myers, *The Eerdmans Bible Dictionary* (Grand Rapids, Mich.: Eerdmans, 1987). 406.

fathers to their children and the hearts of children to their fathers. He turns them away from themselves and to one another by proclaiming the Lamb's arrival for the sins of the world. The great and awesome day of the Lord that John announces and ushers in is none other than the day of our Lord's rejection by the Father, His bloody and innocent sacrifice on our behalf, the Lamb's roasting in His Father's wrath on the cross which was meant for us. The whole point of calling Him the Lamb of God is that He is to be slain as a sacrifice and roasted.

And that, as much as the tender babe in His mother's lap, fills us—the faithful, those who fear the name of the Lord—with the joy of leaping calves. For by it God has made us His people, and our redemption draws near.

In ✠ *Jesus' name. Amen.*

Wednesday of Advent 2

Malachi 3:1-5; 4:5-6
St. Matthew 11:11-15

In the name of the Father and of the ✠ Son and of the Holy Spirit. Amen.

The kingdoms of earth overcome with violence. Glory is won by force. The strong, the proud, and the mighty are rewarded. The kings of the earth rule with armies and weapons. At the first sign of weakness, the vultures and rebels arise to destroy them.

Not so in the kingdom of heaven. It suffers violence. It is the kingdom of martyrs, of the lowly and of the weak; that is a description not only of its citizens but also of its king. Those who lay hold of the kingdom of heaven are those who would suffer violence with and for it. They lay hold of it by a violent separation from the world of violence. They put their hands to plows made from swords and do not look back. They turn the other cheek and suffer violence. They are weak. They are obsessed, caring nothing for anything save this kingdom and its king. This is the picture of faith: the kingdom of heaven suffers violence and the violent take it by force. It is also a picture of the king who suffers violence on the cross as a lamb to the slaughter and who will not respond in kind.

What kind of a God allows Himself to be abused by mortals? What kind of a God suffers violence and dies? Not the kind designed by men, that is for sure. This is not our plan. It doesn't quite seem to have been John the Baptist's plan either. He was the greatest of those born of women, but he might still have doubted. "Are you the coming one or not? Because it looks bad, Lord. It looks like you're not the coming one, but simply a weak man."

What kind of a God is this, who suffers violence, who makes Himself weak, who is born out-of-doors and judged by unjust and petty rulers? What kind of a God takes all the devil's violence onto Himself and doesn't lash out in righteous vengeance and anger?

He is the only kind. He is love and He loves mankind. This love propels Him into our dark world. Out of love, for a while, He denies Himself. He comes in meekness and submission and even suffers violence.

John preached that violence: "Behold the Lamb of God that takes away the sin of the world." That can only mean that Jesus is the fulfillment of the Passover lamb: the Lamb sacrificed, murdered, and roasted to shield His people from the angel of death. "Behold the Lamb of God that takes away the sin of the world" means that He is also the scapegoat who will take our sins out into the wilderness and die alone with them rather than have them held against us.

By the violence done to Christ, the kingdom is won. It is seized by violent men. By it still, by the violent death and resurrection of Jesus Christ, He rules in our hearts. He rules violent men. This is His kingdom of grace, and in us it still suffers violence.

John is our Elijah, foretold by Malachi. Let him turn our hearts to the Father. Let his preaching prepare us for the day of the Lord, and let all the prophets and the Law end in Christ. Our righteousness draws near. Violence is swallowed in grace. The gates of hell, meant to keep us in, hang on their hinges, destroyed and impotent. And heaven has no gates or wall to keep us out. The flaming sword of the cherubim has been extinguished in blood and beaten into a plowshare.

In ☩ Jesus' name. Amen.

Thursday of Advent 2

St. Luke 1:68-79

In the name of the Father and of the ✠ Son and of the Holy Spirit. Amen.

John the Baptist, announcer of the Lamb, was no lamb. He was a pugilist, one to whom peace does not come easily, but only after a long struggle.† He was destined for the wilderness and for martyrdom. He simply couldn't get along in this world. He couldn't behave according to its conventions and niceties.

How much of John's fiery personality and Elijah-like character did Zechariah foresee at his circumcision? I don't know. Yet at that moment, filled with the Holy Spirit, Zechariah prophesied that this prophet of the Most High, John himself—whatever troubles he would have and no matter how unpopular he would be—would guide our feet into the way of peace. Perhaps there would be no peace for John on earth, but he would guide us to it nonetheless.

That guiding comes through John's extreme personality and message. It is the guidance of preparation. John must be incomplete. He is a caricature of a prophet and austerity, for he is not the Christ and he must decrease. He goes before the Lord to prepare His way, not to make the way. He prepares by giving knowledge of salvation in the forgiveness of sins, which is to say, he gives knowledge and recognition of the Messiah. The Lamb he proclaims and prepares for takes away the sin of the world. That sin is taken away because of the tender mercy of our God which has caused the Dawn to visit us, indeed to dwell among us, from on high. John is not the light, but he bears witness to the Light who gives light to those who sit in darkness and in death.

---

† Paraphrased from F. W. Farrar, *The Gospel According to St Luke*, Cambridge Greek Testament for Schools and Colleges (Cambridge: Cambridge University Press, 1893), 106.

In this preparation there is nothing new, but everything old is now full and renewed. This is the way of peace that passes all understanding. The babe in cousin Mary's womb is the fulfillment of every Hebrew greeting: *Shalom*. The oath that the Lord swore to Abraham was nothing else but a promise to be with His people and to be their God. To be their God must mean that He is on their side, that He stands with them against their enemies and those who hate them, chief of which is the devil himself.

So the Messiah is nothing new. He is what was always promised and waited for: He is the horn of salvation for us in the house of David. The rabbis of old, before the generation of John, called Him King Messiah, for they knew that He would restore the kingdom and rule forever.

John proclaims the constant character of the divine message. He repeats what was always in the mouths of the prophets. Their message is his message. The only difference is that there is a body, a man, at the end of John's pointing finger. Where Moses said, "One day the Lamb of God prefigured in these Passover lambs will come," John simply said, "Behold! There He is: the Lamb who points to nothing else, who foreshows and typifies nothing else, but simply is. Behold! There He is: the Lamb who takes away the sin of the world."

That old priest, Zechariah, saw in the old lady's arms his son, a miracle born out of time, circumcised into the promise made to Abraham. He had no expectation to ever play with his grandchildren or see his son grow into adulthood, but he sang for joy nonetheless. Zechariah was passing on, was no longer needed at the temple. His son came ushering in the end of the temple and the Levitical priesthood. So Zechariah sang for joy, not because he had a baby when he was old but because he had a Messiah and the temple service was fulfilled and old age and death were not the end.

The Messiah comes from David's house, but no relatives sit on the throne. The kings are done. And as the temple fades, so do the prophets. We no longer need priests, kings, or prophets. We have the Messiah, born not out of an old, dry womb, but springing forth out of a virgin, a shoot from the stump of Jesse to make children out of Gentiles and to make us leap like newborn calves in spring.

This is what John prepares us for: the way of peace, which is the way of the Lord.

In ☩ Jesus' name. Amen.

FRIDAY OF ADVENT 2

2 Corinthians 3:18-4:5
St. Mark 1:1-8

In the name of the Father and of the ✠ Son and of the Holy Spirit. Amen.

The genesis of the exceedingly good news of Jesus Christ, the Son of God, is written in the prophets Malachi and Isaiah and begins with John the Baptist: "Behold, I send my messenger before your face, who will prepare your way, the voice of one crying in the wilderness: 'Prepare the way of the Lord, make his paths straight.'"

The Isaiah quote will be picked up by John himself. When the Pharisees ask him through proxies what he says of himself, he says, "I am a voice crying in the wilderness: Make straight the way of the Lord." In all three places that this appears in Holy Scripture—in Mark's Gospel as something about John, in the Baptist's own mouth in John's Gospel, and in the original in Isaiah— there is no definite article. Both the King James and our modern translations get that wrong. John is not *the* voice. He is a voice. In part, this is because he is not the only mouthpiece God sent to Israel. But more significantly, it is the one whose paths he is making straight who is *the* voice of God, indeed God Himself.

The Ancient of Days has come to the earth. He has enfleshed Himself out of Mary's womb and has made Himself a man, a human. He has grown up from a little child to manhood, and the beginning of His offer to Israel as King Messiah is a voice crying: "Repent, be baptized, and be forgiven." Those who would tread the Lord's way need preparation. The Lord's way is the hearts of His people, and His people go His way. He seeks to come into them and if they are not made ready, then His entrance will destroy them. So also do they seek to follow Him, but to follow Him is to pick up a cross—and crosses kill people.

Thus John's ministry was to abase the proud and lift up the humble. He prepares people for the Messiah through repentance and forgiveness, that they might receive the Messiah—the Lord in the flesh, who was come to save them—and not be destroyed.

So it is that John still ministers to us today. We still need preparation. The Gospel begun in the wilderness continues now among us. King Messiah, risen from the dead, comes to us hidden in bread and wine, but He is no less dangerous now than He was then. We must be prepared, and we are prepared in the same way: repentance, baptism, and forgiveness. Thus prepared, the coming of Jesus is indeed very good news.

If John is not worthy to unlatch the Lord's sandals, we are not either. Yet John does more than unlatch His sandals; at His insistence, John anoints Him for His office and institutes the sacrament of Holy Baptism. Thus are we, in Holy Baptism, joined to the Messianic office. And though we are not any more worthy to unlatch His sandals than John was, He baptizes with the Holy Spirit, thus elevating us to His own home and family. He makes us not simply friends and brothers but deigns to call us bride and beloved and temple.

In ✠ Jesus' name. Amen.

Saturday of Advent 2

Romans 15:4-13

In the name of the Father and of the ✠ Son and of the Holy Spirit. Amen.

Christ our Lord was Himself circumcised. In this way He became a servant to the circumcised. He submitted to the knife that cut the covenant with Abraham, putting Himself into the place of sinners who need blood to cover their sins and God's grace to bring them into His family. He did this to show God's truthfulness and to confirm the promises given to the patriarchs. But St. Paul tells us that He also did this in order that Gentiles might glorify God for His mercy.

The truth about God is that His mercy endures forever. He desires mercy, not sacrifice. Thus He meets the demands of sacrifice, the cost and consequence of our sins, in Himself for the sake of being merciful, in order to spare Jews and Gentiles alike the punishment their sins deserved. His consistency and character to Abraham and the circumcised, even His willingness to suffer in this way, allows the Gentiles to glorify God for His mercy. For the uncircumcised believer sees in the circumcision of Jesus Christ that God keeps His promises and will not stop short of delivering His people from death. Indeed, for this purpose, He will suffer even worse violence and shame than that of circumcision.

To demonstrate how this is also for the Gentiles, St. Paul quotes Isaiah: "The root of Jesse will come, even he who arises to rule the Gentiles; in him will the Gentiles hope."

The Lord rules the Gentiles as He ruled Abraham. Abraham believed and it was reckoned unto him as righteousness. The God of Abraham is enthroned on praise, and that praise springs forth from the forgiveness of sins in those who believe that God is merciful and forgives their sins. He rules in mercy by becoming Father to the children that

He raises up, if He must, out of stones. And those children are filled with hope and praise for Him.

Repentance and faith is the journey from God as judge to God as Father. Hope is the expectation that God's promises are true and that there is room for Gentiles, that even they might be bold enough to call Him Lord and Father.

This isn't just for Gentiles, then, for the Samaritan woman and the faithful centurion. There is room for you, no matter who your mother was. Stop thinking that you are so unique, so special, and so complicated in your sins and your situation that God has to make some special allowance for you or that you might be the exception to the rule. Repent. Your sins aren't that spectacular or shocking. Repent and stop trying to be the center of attention. Repent and bask in the simple promise that the Lord didn't leave anyone out, not even you. Calm down and rejoice. He was circumcised to show God's truthfulness, to confirm the promises to the patriarchs, that you might glorify Him for His mercy.

Faith expects that God is good and merciful. It trusts in the truth of His mercy. It allows Him to be the Savior and is happy to simply receive the credit and blessing of God without a big fuss about how thankful it is or how much God overcame. Faith basks in peace.

This, then, is the blessing that God places upon you through St. Paul: "May the God of hope fill you with all joy and peace in believing, so that by the power of the Holy Spirit you may abound in hope."

In ✠ *Jesus' name. Amen.*

The Third Sunday in Advent

Isaiah 40:1-11
1 Corinthians 4:1-5
St. Matthew 11:2-11

In the name of the Father and of the ✠ Son and of the Holy Spirit. Amen.

When John was in prison and knew that the end of his life was imminent, when it seemed as though the kingdom had failed and the satan Herod would win, he sent word by his disciples for a final word from Jesus. He is asking for assurance and puts it rather bluntly, but he is also throwing down a gauntlet: "Are you the coming one, or do we wait for another?"

Typical of Jesus, He knows better than John what John needs, and He is patient and kind to His impatient children. He does not, however, say "yes." He does not say, "It will be well with you, John. You go to the prophet's reward. Fear not, for I know what I am doing." He says, "The blind receive their sight and the lame walk, lepers are cleansed and the deaf hear, and the dead are raised up, and the poor have good news preached to them."

Jesus directs John to the Scriptures. If John wants assurance that Jesus is the coming one, the Messiah, then he needs to look to the promises. Man lives not by bread alone, but by every word that proceeds from the mouth of God. In particular, Jesus is directing John to Isaiah 35:

> Strengthen the weak hands,
>   and make firm the feeble knees.
> Say to those who have an anxious heart,
>   "Be strong; fear not!
> Behold, your God
>   will come with vengeance,

with the recompense of God.
He will come and save you."
Then the eyes of the blind shall be opened,
and the ears of the deaf unstopped;
then shall the lame man leap like a deer,
and the tongue of the mute sing for joy.
For waters break forth in the wilderness,
and streams in the desert.
(Isa. 35:3-6)

Isaiah says, "Your God will come and save you" and *then* "the eyes of the blind shall be opened, and the ears of the deaf unstopped." John should look and see what is happening. Yet he should not take comfort so much in the signs themselves, but in the Word and promises of God. The key thing is this: "Your God will come and save you," not "the blind will see and the lepers will be cleansed." The key thing is that God keeps His Word and the faithful wait, in faith, for the day when there will be no blind or deaf, lame or leprous.

So, too, then John should look to his own office. A few chapters later Isaiah gives John his duties:

Comfort, comfort my people,
says your God.
Speak tenderly to Jerusalem,
and cry to her
that her warfare is ended,
that her iniquity is pardoned,
that she has received from the LORD's hand
double for all her sins.

A voice cries:
"In the wilderness prepare the way of the LORD;
make straight in the desert a highway for our God.
Every valley shall be lifted up,
and every mountain and hill be made low;

the uneven ground shall become level,
 and the rough places a plain.
And the glory of the LORD shall be revealed,
 and all flesh shall see it together,
 for the mouth of the LORD has spoken."
 (Isa. 40:1-5)

The coming one is the Lord Himself, Yahweh. John doesn't prepare for another fallen and fallible man in office, for a prophet, a priest, or a king. He prepares the way for the Lord Himself, for our God. What he prepares is the hearts of men. What he prepares them for is the Lord, for the one who led the people out of Egypt, the one who brought the people back from Babylon, the one who walked in the garden seeking reconciliation with Adam and Eve. He prepares the hearts of men for the Lord with tender words of comfort and a declaration of peace, even though it comes out and hits the itchy ears of men as a harsh call to repentance: "Listen up, O people of God: Your warfare with God, your long rebellion and self-destruction, is ended. Your guilt is pardoned. Your sins are forgiven. The Lord has taken it upon Himself to stand in your stead and face the accusations and endure the tortures of hell that were due you in order to spare you and to welcome you back to Himself."

That is the Lord's glory. It is revealed to those with eyes to see, not in shows of might or power nor in the healing of the lame and raising of the dead, but in the preaching of the good news of peace in Christ. It is revealed there until such time as the Lord returns in glory on the last day and there are no more blind or deaf, lame or leprous. And even that glory, the glory of the last day, is revealed and known most fully when He is lifted up from the earth. And even John, greatest of the prophets, must constantly be reminded that the Lamb comes to be sacrificed for the sins of the world and not to take the world by force.

There is a sense in which we are all languishing in prison, subject to little and greater Herods, for we have given ourselves to our passions. We have indulged our fleshly desires. We have harbored grudges and jealousies. We have secretly hated and openly gossiped and lied about nearly everything. Everyone who sins is a prisoner of his lust. Repent and hear the Word of the Lord: "'Be strong; fear not! Behold, your God will come with vengeance, with the recompense of God. He will come and save you.' Then the eyes of the blind shall be opened, and the ears of the deaf unstopped; then shall the lame man leap like a deer, and the tongue of the mute sing for joy. For waters break forth in the wilderness, and streams in the desert." And God baptizes for Himself a people who were no people and sets free the prisoners. He is the coming one who has come for you.

In ✠ *Jesus' name. Amen.*

Monday of Advent 3

Psalm 85

In the name of the Father and of the ✠ Son and of the Holy Spirit. Amen.

> *"I will hear what God the Lord will speak: for he will speak peace unto his people, and to his saints."* (Ps. 85:8 KJV)

Once we hid for shame in the garden. We tried to cover our nakedness by our own powers. We fell into sin by contradicting God's Word, and in our sin we did not want to hear it again. So we ran and we hid; we applied fig leaves for shame and in the vain hope that they could protect us from slapping branches and thorns. But God in His patience sought us out. He spoke kindly to us and restored us with a promise. He severed us from the sons of Satan. We do not belong to him. And He joined Himself to our cause in the virginal womb of Eve's offspring Mary, making Himself the enmity between Satan and us.

So it is that the saints of God, the baptized and redeemed who hope in Christ, are now, by His grace, eager for the Word of God. With the sons of Korah they are bold to say: *I will hear what God the Lord will speak: for he will speak peace unto his people, and to his saints.*

God's consistent grace and promise have taught us to expect peace from Him. In that expectation and hope, we love His Word and are eager for it.

Let us then consider three aspects of this Word. In the first place, the Word of God is eternal and uncreated: "In the beginning was the Word" (John 1:1). We receive it, that which called all things to be, as the very power of God unto salvation. Only that which is eternal can undo our eternal punishment and establish eternal peace for us. The eternal Word has entered time, has become flesh for us, and because of that—the very fulfillment of the promise made first to Eve—we are bold to say: *I will hear what God the* L*ORD* *will speak: for he will speak peace unto his people, and to his saints.*

This eternal Word, which was in the beginning, which is uncreated, took up our flesh and is the very Prince of Peace. He is announced by angels to shepherds with the greeting of peace. He greets His disciples on the eve of His resurrection with peace. And when He says, "Peace be with you," it is more than a pious wish or meaningless greeting. It is a promise.

I will hear what God the L*ORD* *will speak: for he will speak peace unto his people, and to his saints.*

In the second place, the Word of God is given by inspiration and not by the cleverness of men. We also receive this by faith.

> All scripture is given by inspiration of God, and is profitable for doctrine, for reproof, for correction, for instruction in righteousness. (2 Tim. 3:16 KJV)

> Sanctify them through thy truth: thy word is truth. (John 17:17 KJV)

> But the Comforter, which is the Holy Ghost, whom the Father will send in my name, he shall teach you all things, and bring all things to your remembrance, whatsoever I have said unto you. (John 14:26 KJV)

Thus are we comforted that God's Word is true and trustworthy. By it every evil is overcome and every good bestowed. In this comfort we are freed from both doubt and fear. We have peace because the Word of God is solid and endures forever.

I will hear what God the L*ORD* *will speak: for he will speak peace unto his people, and to his saints.*

Finally, God's Word is vocal. We receive the Word of God by faith, out loud, in preaching.

> Man shall not live by bread alone, but by every word that proceedeth out of the mouth of God. (Matt. 4:4 KJV)

> He that hath ears to hear, let him hear. (Luke 8:8 KJV)

> [H]e that believeth in me, though he were dead, yet shall he live. (John 11:25 KJV)

> Speak, LORD; for thy servant heareth. (1 Sam. 3:9 KJV)

The Lord doesn't think nice things in our general direction. He speaks and we hear. "He who hears you, hears Me," says the Lord. Thus our peace is guaranteed. It is delivered in objective means outside of ourselves. And we are as bold as the sons of Korah to confess: *I will hear what God the LORD will speak: for he will speak peace unto his people, and to his saints.*†

In ✠ Jesus' name. Amen.

---

† Some of the ideas and verses for this sermon were found in *Thomas Aquinas, Ninety-Nine Homilies of S. Thomas Aquinas Upon the Epistles and Gospels for Forty-Nine Sundays of the Christian Year*, trans. John M. Ashley, vol. 3 (London: Church Press Company, 1867), 18-19.

Tuesday of Advent 3

Isaiah 40:1-11

In the name of the Father and of the ✠ Son and of the Holy Spirit. Amen.

The Lord says to Isaiah: "Comfort, comfort my people ... Speak tenderly to Jerusalem, and cry to her that her warfare is ended, that her iniquity is pardoned, that she has received from the Lord's hand double for all her sins" (Isa. 40:1-2).

The historical context for this can be a bit confusing because when Isaiah tells Jerusalem that her warfare is ended, she isn't at war. He is speaking to the people of Jerusalem who will be carried off to exile in Babylon before it happens. This, of course, is impossible for the critics to believe, but it is not so difficult for us. For we believe both in inspired prophecy which foretells the future and also in the constant character of God's comforting words to sinners.

Isaiah foretells that a war not yet begun with Babylon will end and that Judah's iniquity will be pardoned. She will be brought back from captivity. This certainly jibes with our Lord's own sentiment and statement to the disciples in John 14: "And now I have told you before it come to pass, that, when it is come to pass, ye might believe" (v. 29 KJV). But more than simply proving that God warned them of the danger of their sin, it is meant to comfort the captives. The Lord's "anger endureth but a moment; in his favour is life: weeping may endure for a night, but joy cometh in the morning" (Ps. 30:5 KJV).

The Law serves the Gospel. Already in the garden, the Lord delayed the physical death of Adam, that the Messianic line might be established and Adam spared the eternal death he deserved. So also, immediately after the golden calf apostasy in Exodus 32, the Lord revealed to Moses that He is "merciful and gracious, longsuffering, and abundant in goodness and truth" (Exod. 34:6 KJV). As Isaiah looks ahead to what will happen to Jerusalem, he recognizes that the horrible suffering of the Babylonian captivity is God's alien work and that His proper work and desire is to comfort His people and restore them to His fellowship.†

That is why the words ring true for the Jerusalem of Isaiah's day, even though those people aren't carried from Jerusalem, and also why they ring true for us. God desires to speak tenderly to us. He knows that our hearts are broken, that we have been brutalized by Satan and his demons, by the world, and by our fallen flesh. He knows that we are not at home here, that we are not safe here, and that we are lonely. So He tells His prophets—not just Isaiah and not just John but everyone who is set into office to bring His Word to His people—He tells them to comfort His people, to hush her cries of despair, to tell her not to be afraid, that her warfare is ended and her iniquity pardoned, that she has done more than enough and received double for all her sins.

So far all the Lutherans are tracking just fine, but what about that last bit? You have received double for all your sins? How so? Jerusalem didn't pay double for all her sins, not even close. The wages of sin is death. She didn't die twice. She didn't even die once. As bad as Babylon was, she didn't endure anything that is really worthy of comparison to an eternity in hell. But the prophet is instructed to tell her that has received double for all her sins.

But it is true. It is true because she shouldn't have paid or suffered at all. Her iniquity is pardoned. She has no sins in God's ledger. The account has been paid in full by the Messiah who has suffered in her stead. How dare anyone, even the Lord Himself, charge her for sins? Any sorrow, any discomfort, is more than should be paid.

The economy of heaven doesn't make any sense to fallen accountants: double comfort for each sin. The forgiveness of God in Christ is

---

† R. Reed Lessing, *Isaiah 40-55: Concordia Commentary* (St. Louis: Concordia Publishing House, 2011), 132.

so great that it doesn't simply eliminate the debt and call things even, but it bestows a balance. So if you cheated and stole from God $1,000 worth of stuff, rather simply forgiving the debt, He gives you $1,000 more.

Here is the hope of God's people: the Lord is "merciful and gracious, longsuffering, and abundant in goodness and truth." Even when their sinful bodies are failing, even when they must face the judge and all the world seems unjust, even when they have brought suffering on themselves through their sins, the Lord's people have this: the war is over. Heaven is on your side. Your iniquity is pardoned. No one, not even God, can charge you for your sins.

In ✠ Jesus' name. Amen.

Ember Wednesday in Advent

Isaiah 2:2-5; 7:10-15
St. Luke 1:26-38

In the name of the Father and of the ✠ Son and of the Holy Spirit. Amen.

The Virgin conceives and bears a Son, a Savior, Emmanuel. He is a sign against Ahaz and a sign against all fallen men, beginning with Adam. That is not how we are used to hearing the verse, but it is true. The virginal conception of Jesus Christ is a sign against our impotence, our standing idly by while Eve is seduced.

So it is that not only are we sinful, but everything we conceive is full of sin—even, saddest of all, our children. So also does everything that we conceive die. Our malice and greed, our lust and violence are passed on to our children. And those sins kill them.

Ahaz had his plans, and he had good reason to be afraid for his life and for his country. So he conceived a strategy that would make a corrupt politician proud. He would play his enemies against one another. He would outsmart them. He would not ask God for a sign because he didn't trust God to give what he needed. He didn't need platitudes about trust and letting go. He figured that what he needed were real and pragmatic things, and God simply couldn't be trusted to give him those things. The steel of Syria's swords was not imaginary or hypothetical. Thus he refused a sign. He rejected God's Word. He rejected it because he did not want God to interfere with his plans.

Repent! God is weary of men who feign piety, who rely upon philosophy and man's wisdom to excuse themselves for their lack of faith and for their evil deeds. He is weary of men who twist His Word to bring it into conformity with modern sensibilities, who dismiss His Word as meaningless and impractical fluff. Repent, O fearful men, who mock God with your "theology" and excuses.

The spirit of Ahaz is still with us. We are still tempted to his pretend piety. There is a pretend piety for those who claim they have a passion for the lost, and there is a pretend piety as well for those who claim to love doctrine and the liturgy. There is a pretend piety for every sinful man ever born. One is not better than another, and do not think that God will wink at yours or not mind it as much as another's. Repent.

And also rejoice. That for which Ahaz would not ask, God gave, and it was better than Ahaz, or even Abraham for that matter, could have imagined or hoped. God conceives a Son in the Virgin's womb to rescue men not merely from a pagan oppressor, a military conqueror and enslaver, but from the devil himself. He is a sign against our impotence, but also for our salvation.

Despite our lies, rebellion, and hatred, in contrast to our theology, philosophy, and pragmatism, God is with us. He has taken up our flesh. He wears our skin. He moves about with the muscles, bones, and cartilage of a man, conceived in one of us. He has a body like ours, taken from the Virgin's womb. And like our bodies, His body is bruised and dying, indeed, was created for the very purpose of being bruised and crucified. He has a human soul as well, for He is an actual man. His soul was created for the sole purpose that it be separated from His body, that He endure physical death in our place and be set Adam-like, dust to dust, into the ground. He is one of us, in life and in death. He is with us. He is Emmanuel who lives our life and dies our death.

Here is a sign for Ahaz: the Lord has come in the flesh into this dreary and deadly plain to join our cause, make us His, and deliver us from Assyria and hell. In this way, by the sign Ahaz refused, He is our Savior and has met the enemy's attack in Himself. In dying, He has broken down the prison bars that held us in. Hell swallowed Him and can take no more. He bursts it like new wine in an old wine skin. In rising, He has paved the way to heaven. For if He lived our life and died our death, so also has He risen our resurrection.

All this the Lord has done, not because we asked or because we believed or had the facts and details right, but because He is good and His mercy endureth forever and He gives a sign to those who refuse. He has died our death and instituted our resurrection and ascended in our ascension. Thus He has elevated our nature to the Father's right hand, for He is still our Emmanuel. He is with us.

Of course, He is still, and forever, God. What we seem prone to forget, however, is that even now, even after the resurrection and ascension, He is still and forever man. He has ascended as a man and sits at the Father's right as a man, and yet is still with us. For now that He has fulfilled His Father's will, He does not deny Himself His divine rights and attributes as a man. And so He is, as a man, capable of more than one mode of presence. He can be there as a man and also with us, as a man, in His body and blood in the Holy Communion and also present in His Word. He is Jacob's ladder. But we don't climb up on Him to heaven; He brings heaven down to us.

And Ahaz, wherever he raises up his head, will not stop Him. This sign—the Virgin conceiving and bearing a Son, our Emmanuel, God with us—will not be stopped by vanity, violence, or lies. He has conquered sin and has conquered Ahaz as surely as He has conquered Assyria and Babylon.

All the children of God, all believers, are thus conceived. What we conceive is full of sin and dies, but what God conceives rises and ascends. All God's children go the way of Christ. St. Mary the Virgin is your mother, for Christ is surely your brother. You were not born by the will of a man. You were born in water and in Word, born from above, and by His grace you are now virgin-pure, even as He—your bridegroom and your brother—is.

And you will follow Him, not just in the way of the cross (though you will drink the cup He drank) because that is neither the end nor the goal. You will follow Him in the resurrection and the ascension to come. For lo, He is Emmanuel. He is with you always.

In ✠ Jesus' name. Amen.

Thursday of Advent 3

St. Luke 2:29-32

In the name of the Father and of the ✠ Son and of the Holy Spirit. Amen.

The Nunc Dimittis is the most familiar of all the canticles since we normally sing it after the distribution of the Holy Communion. Familiarity doesn't always breed contempt. Sometimes it simply breeds inattention and taking-for-grantedness. Let us then strive to hear Simeon's song anew:

> Lord, now lettest thou thy servant depart in peace, according to thy word: for mine eyes have seen thy salvation, which thou hast prepared before the face of all people; a light to the lighten the Gentiles, and the glory of thy people Israel. (Luke 2:29-32 KJV)

The word translated here as *Lord* is not the word *Kyrie*. *Kyrie* is the New Testament word for *YHWH*. It is almost always freighted with allusions and reminders of who Christ is according to the prophets and how He has acted in the history of Israel. Here the word is the cognate of our word *despot*. The best translation is probably *king* or *ruler* or *master*. The set-up is not as friendly as it sounds in English because the word usually translated as *servant* happens to mean *slave*. Here is the point: Simeon stands in the temple as a slave speaking to his master.

We also have a bit of a problem with "let your servant depart." It is more active than that. Simeon is actually asking the Lord to send him away. It is not the master allowing his slave to leave at his leisure, but the master actively sending him away. But even that is not quite enough, for this is the word that is used for the release of a soldier from his duties. The soldier is dismissed from the war, relieved of his duties, and sent home. It also the word used for divorce. A wife is freed from her abusive husband and sent back to her loving parents. Most significantly, however, the word is used for the freeing of a slave who had been captured in war after his ransom has been paid by his family. So "let your servant depart" just doesn't quite cut it.

The key thing, however, is not that the Master is now sending His slave Simeon away in freedom, which He certainly is, but that He is sending him in peace. The Master is releasing him, to be sure; Simeon's bondage to the Law, to his duties, and to watching in the temple are complete. But He is not simply sending him away because the relationship is over and Simeon has paid his dues. The master is elevating the slave to become a peer in the realm. He goes not as a freed slave, but in the king's peace. He goes as a prince, as a friend of the king, with the king's blessing and approval.

This peace and elevating and freeing are because Simeon's eyes have seen the Master's salvation—not Simeon's salvation, but the Master's. That salvation is the baby Jesus. That is what Simeon's eyes have seen; that is what his arms are holding.

And if that wasn't enough, then comes the real surprise: the Master has prepared this baby before the face of all people in order to elevate and free slaves who were no people, or who were His enemies, to be His people. He prepared this baby through the prophets. There the Master revealed the mission and the motivation behind the Messiah, behind this baby. He—the person of Jesus Christ, the baby in Simeon's arms—is the glory of Israel because He reveals the Master's true character to the Gentiles, that is, to God's ancient enemies.

His true character is definitely a surprise because, at first glance, He appears to be a brutal master. He enslaves people! He is the Law-giver who placed the cherubim with flaming swords at the east edge of Eden to keep us out. He is the God who opened up the earth and swallowed Korah and his rebels. He is the God who rebuked His people through Babylon with torture and exile.

And yet, as foretold in the prophets, He is the suffering servant who lays down His life to buy back rebels who hate Him. He is the God who goes to the marketplace and buys back his wife Gomer who sold herself into prostitution against Him. He is the God who seeks Adam and Eve in the garden even though they don't seek Him.

The forgiving and gracious character of Yahweh is in every word of the prophets, but it is slowly unwrapped through the ages. It is made more clear as each prophet expands and expounds upon his predecessors. It becomes more clear again when the Virgin conceives, when Jesus is brought to the temple, and when He is baptized and begins to teach. But it is most clear, and becomes even obvious, even to Gentiles like us, when Jesus is crucified as the sacrifice for the sins of the world and rises from the dead so that we might look upon and partake of His body and blood.

That is why, with the body and blood of Jesus still upon our breath, we are bold to sing with Simeon: "Lord, now lettest thou thy servant depart in peace."

In ✠ Jesus' name. Amen.

Ember Friday in Advent

Isaiah 11:1-5
St. Luke 1:39-47

In the name of the Father and of the ✠ Son and of the Holy Spirit. Amen.

B lessed is she who believed, for there will be a fulfillment of those things which were told her from the Lord," said St. Elizabeth to St. Mary.

St. Mary was just pregnant. The Holy Spirit had overshadowed her, and she had conceived. The seed of Abraham was in her womb. He was a child without a father even as He was a priest without a genealogy. She was probably not showing yet, but she was probably scared. Her parents may have even sent her there out of shame while they tried to figure out what to do. St. Joseph had come close to dismissing her, but Gabriel told him the score and he, in faith like Mary's, believed and kept his word. Maybe that is why Mary's folks eventually let her come home.

Whatever the circumstances, Elizabeth rejoiced to see her. She told her that the pregnancy was good, nothing to be ashamed of, but that for which to be exceedingly thankful. That is not true of every pregnancy, but it was true of this one. And Elizabeth says it out loud. She honors Mary and calls her the mother of the Lord. What a relief it must have been to hear what the angel said confirmed in a human voice, to be reminded once again that the things she was told would be fulfilled. She would bear the holy child, the Savior of the world. She would be the most blessed of all women. She would be redeemed from all her sins. Her shame and sorrows would all be removed. Blessed is she who believed, for there will be a fulfillment of those things which were told her from the Lord.

This is also true for you. Blessed are you who believe. There will be a fulfillment of those things which you have been told by the Lord.

What has the Lord told you? He has told you, "I baptize you in the name of the Father and of the Son and of the Holy Spirit." He has told you, "I forgive you all your sins." He has told you, "Take, eat. This is My body. Take, drink. This cup is the New Testament in My blood." You are innocent. You are holy. You are clean, pure, immaculate, complete. The life, suffering, death, and resurrection of Jesus Christ stand in your place. All His good and perfect works are credited to your account, and God is well-pleased with and delights in you.

But it may not feel that way. Like a woman just pregnant, it may not show. But it will be fulfilled. It is true already, whether or not it feels like it or shows. You have been overshadowed by the Holy Spirit. Jesus abides in you. You belong to Him. You will be freed from all this pain, sorrow, and shame. What God has said to and about you is truer than what you or your neighbors see.

Mary's sorrows were just beginning when she met the pregnant Elizabeth. The shame of her pregnancy and of Jesus' ignoble, out-of-doors birth would only increase in the following year until she had to flee in the night from Herod's soldiers and be exiled for a time in Egypt. Eventually she would come home, but nothing would be the same. She'd also lose Joseph along the way. Then she would stand at the foot of the cross in horror as they tortured and mocked her friendless Son. A sword would pierce her heart, and she would know sorrow like no other mother on earth.

But she would also see the risen Lord, and even in her sorrows she knew joy. She is the most blessed of women. The covenant with Abraham is fulfilled through her womb. What she was told and believed is fulfilled. She gets it right in her sung response to Elizabeth's prophecy. She praises God for how He has treated her, for His mercy and strength as evidenced in His historic grace to His people, for His consideration of the poor and the meek, and for the giving of His seed, the Savior of all men.

That good news is what sees her through, what comforts her in the night, what she waits for during her long years on earth even after His ascension. Again, it is the same for you. She is a type of you. She lives out your faith.

She is also an example, for once a certain woman from the crowd raised her voice and said to Jesus, "Blessed is the womb that bore You, and the breasts which nursed You!" That is, "Blessed is St. Mary." That is true. She is the most blessed of all women. But Jesus said, "More than that, blessed are those who hear the word of God and keep it!"

Blessed are you who hear the Word of God and love it. What has caused this love of theology, of hymnody, of the Word, in you? It does not come on its own, from within you. It is the Spirit. Do not be fooled by your doubts and besetting sins. It is faith born from above that has brought you here this morning.

Blessed is she who believed. Blessed are you who hear.

In ✠ Jesus' name. Amen.

EMBER SATURDAY IN ADVENT

Isaiah 19:20-22; 35:1-7; 40:9-11; 45:1-8
Daniel 3:52-56 (Apocrypha)
2 Thessalonians 2:1-8
St. Luke 3:1-6

In the name of the Father and of the ✠ Son and of the Holy Spirit. Amen.

The hearts of the faithful all over the world are these days pondering the mystery of God lying in weakness and poverty in a manger. That weakness and poverty brings us deep, abiding joy.

The festivities of this season are mindless fun when times are good. They have their place. But you don't need me to tell you that when times turn bad, when your mother dies at Christmas, or you face your first Christmas since losing your father, that the mindless fun of the season mainly loses its fun. That is what makes this time of year depressing for so many. It is never quite what we think it should, or wish it would, be. We long for our lost childhood, for the times when we had not so many loved ones buried in the earth; when we had not yet suffered so many betrayals and heartaches at the hands of those we love; when our lives didn't have so much to regret, so many mistakes and selfish acts; when Christmas seemed a time of endless possibility and magic.

By definition, nostalgia is always sad. But the happiness of Santa and his elves just doesn't cut it when you're alone or when you discover it is all imaginary. Nor do thoughts of how happy you once were or almost were bring comfort. Just about everybody over the age of twelve or so is going to suffer from this.

But here is a spiritual trick. Instead of turning inward and moping about or trying extra hard to be Martha Stewart, heed the call of John in the desert. You are sad. You have a sack full of regrets. You long for a more innocent time and your loved ones back from the dead. You

61

wish you were younger, healthier? Then repent. Because what you are feeling is the weight of the curse, of the Law, of death. The best answer to seasonal depression is the voice crying in the wilderness.

Turn not to some quick fix or easy answer, but to the Church's joy, to the angels' joy, to Mary's and the shepherds' joy. That joy is joy in the midst of poverty and hardship. It is joy at the birth of Jesus Christ, of God becoming flesh, pleased to be a man and to go to hell for men, that men would not pay for their sins or die eternally. It is the answer to the curse, the end of our rebellion, and the pledge of the reunion to come.

That joy is not fleeting or simple. It is complicated, deep, and it co-exists alongside of pain and regret, even as faith co-exists alongside of doubt. This is not the happy fun of squealing children or sugar plums. It is different, deeper and more satisfying, if not quite so exciting, but it also more abiding.

There is time for sugar plums, for feasting, and for children's laughter. Thank God for all of that. But do not think that those things are the goal or end of our faith. We aren't going to a circus in heaven to be entertained like Caesar's citizens. We are going to worship the Father, in perfect communion with the Lamb and the Spirit. St. John stands in the desert and points to the end of our faith, to our hope, to our joy: Behold the Lamb of God who takes away the sin of the world. He calls us to repentance, not sadness. Repentance is sorrow over sin, but it is also confidence and expectation in God's mercy. His baptism is a baptism of repentance for the forgiveness of sins.

Unto us a Savior is born. Turn from nostalgia, from backward-looking and longing, and turn toward the coming of the Messiah on the last day. Turn to the promise, to the future, to the time when our joy will no longer be tempered by death and sadness. Have yourself a John the Baptist Christmas, that is, a Christmas focused upon the Lamb who is risen from the dead.

In ✠ Jesus' name. Amen.

The Fourth Sunday in Advent

Deuteronomy 18:15-19
Philippians 4:4-7
St. John 1:19-28

In the name of the Father and of the ✠ Son and of the Holy Spirit. Amen.

Who are you? You are not the Christ. That is what matters. You are not the Christ, but there is a Christ: there is a Messiah, God born into our world as a man, anointed by the Father in the Jordan's scummy water, the promised coming one. There is a Christ. That is what matters, and that is what defines you.

He, the Christ, felt the sting of Pilate's lash. He bore a crown of thorns. He had the flesh of His hands and feet ripped by nails which held Him to the accursed tree made into the tree of life. O blessed cross, from whence comes all our joy! O fruited wood that delivers the elixir of life. There is a Christ!

John prepared His way with a baptism of repentance for the forgiveness of sins, a bestowal of God's name upon sinful men made clean by grace. There is a Christ. He is the one in David's line who made Bathsheba into a virgin bride and Rahab into a pillar of the community. There is a Christ. He is the one who made deceiving sons of Jacob into His own tribes and elect, a people who were no people, and He brought them through the sea on dry ground.

He is the Christ, your Christ, your God in your flesh, your kinsman-redeemer born and anointed to die for you. He is Jesus of Nazareth, born out-of-doors, rejected by His relatives, hunted by Herod. He is the Lamb of God whose blood shields you from the angel of death, who is exiled into the wilderness to die for your sins.

Who are you? You are not Him. You are not the Christ. But you are a Christian, and you are a Christian because there is a Christ. You are baptized. You wear His name. You are washed in His blood. You eat His flesh, hear His Word, pray His prayers, die His death, and live His life.

You are named not John or Zechariah or Malachi. You are named with baptism: Father, Son, and Holy Spirit. That is the name that was placed upon you. You are not the Christ. You are not God. But God's name is given to you, for you. He gives you His name as a bridegroom gives his bride a name. That holy name opens heaven's gates. It drives away the demons. It banishes guilt, fear, and shame to hell's deepest pit. You belong to the royal court of heaven. You are not the Christ, but you are His.

Hell has lost its claim. Death has lost its victory. God has hands and feet to pierce. God has a brow to wear the thorns and a back to suffer the lash. God has eyes to weep and a mouth to forgive those who kill Him. Hell has no strength, no violence left. The holy life, death, and resurrection of Jesus Christ have taken care of that. Hell's fire, demands, and accusations have all been met and spent until there is no more. There is then no list of your sins, no balance to be paid. The Savior of the nations has crushed the devil's head with His bruised heel. He has paid the ransom in full and more.

Now, we do not put a statue of a baby in the manger because we think that Jesus is still in the manger. We put a statue in the manger to remember that Jesus was a baby, that He took up our flesh and our burden. An empty manger just won't do. The fact that God has a body, was born of a woman, for us, is not a tiny detail in the story or somehow not the important part. It is the essence of the story.

In the same way, we do not put a statue of Jesus on the cross because we think that He is not risen. We know and we rejoice that He is risen. But an empty cross just won't do. The fact that He was crucified in His body is not just a detail or somehow the prelude to the more significant

64

event. It is the essence of the story. We preach Christ crucified. And Hollywood gets this exactly right: the crucifix drives off vampires.

The cross of Jesus Christ, the innocent suffering for the sins of the world, has satisfied all that justice demanded. Neither the devil nor vampires, nor any monsters of any form or depraved imagination, nor real human beings or primordial fears have any claim upon you. They cannot stand against God giving Himself on the cross to have you. The cross is the terror of all your enemies and the joy of all Christendom.

There is a Christ. He has a body. He was born of Mary. He was crucified under Pontius Pilate. He rose and came in that body into the upper room to speak peace upon His disciples. He comes still in that body. He comes to us in His risen body in the Holy Communion to forgive our sins, to shield us from the angel of death, and to unite us to Himself. It is not a metaphor or an allegory. He actually does what He says. He gives His risen body to you to eat, that you be one with Him in holiness and righteousness and that you remember Him and proclaim His holy death.

There is a Christ. He has a body. In Him you are safe. His cross drives off death. His holy life and His holy sacrifice stand between you and hell. You are not the Christ, but thanks be to God, you don't need to be. There is a Christ for you. This Christ defines you even as He names and feeds you. He is what matters.

So it is that the holy Church in her wisdom has asked us today, the Sunday before Christmas, to ponder the question put to John: "Who are you?" That we would not be defined by our names or who sits around our tables or how much loot we rake in this Christmas or by any other way, the Church teaches us this: we belong to Christ. Thus does John himself prepare our hearts and minds for the holy commemoration of God's incarnation, His taking of a body, on Christmas.

In ✠ Jesus' name. Amen.

Monday of Advent 4

Psalm 19

In the name of the Father and of the ✠ Son and of the Holy Spirit. Amen.

The Introit gives us most of the first six verses of Psalm 19. It is a description of the natural Law, that is, what God reveals of Himself through nature apart from His Word.

David sings:

> The heavens declare the glory of God;
> and the firmament sheweth his handywork.
> Day unto day uttereth speech,
> and night unto night sheweth knowledge.
> There is no speech nor language,
> where their voice is not heard.
> Their line is gone out through all the earth,
> and their words to the end of the world.
> In them hath he set a tabernacle for the sun,
> which is as a bridegroom coming out of his chamber,
> and rejoiceth as a strong man to run a race.
> His going forth is from the end of the heaven,
> and his circuit unto the ends of it:
> and there is nothing hid from the heat thereof.
> (Ps. 19:1-6 KJV)

This is a poetic description of the stars. The stars proclaim God's glory. Their arrangement and beauty show that He is a craftsman. They also serve as a tent for the sun, which comes out as a bridegroom from his chamber and like a man running a race across the sky. Even as nothing on earth can fail to hear the sound of the Lord's glory in the sight of the stars, neither can anything on earth escape the heat of the sun. This glory, glorious as it is, cannot save humans.

But David has more to say. He moves from the natural Law to the goodness of the revealed will of God in His Word. He sings:

> The law of the LORD is perfect,
>   converting the soul:
> the testimony of the LORD is sure,
>   making wise the simple.
> The statutes of the LORD are right,
>   rejoicing the heart:
> the commandment of the LORD is pure,
>   enlightening the eyes.
> The fear of the LORD is clean,
>   enduring for ever:
> the judgments of the LORD are true
>   and righteous altogether.
> More to be desired are they than gold,
>   yea, than much fine gold:
> sweeter also than honey
>   and the honeycomb.
>   (Ps. 19:7-10 KJV)

The written Word, the statutes of the Lord, instructs in morality. What the Lord gives is right and good. So also do the statutes of the Lord convert the souls of men and enlighten them. The written Word reveals God's gracious character and the promised Messiah. It shows God's patience and steadfast mercy. What David here calls the Law of the Lord is what Lutheran dogmaticians call the broad use of the term. Here Law means both Law and Gospel or the whole counsel of God. What God gives through this Law is more desirable than any material thing and more glorious than what the stars alone can proclaim.

Next David moves to the Law's theological purpose. Old-time Lutherans learned this as the second use of the Law. David sings:

> Moreover by them is thy servant warned:
>   and in keeping of them there is great reward.

Who can understand his errors?
  Cleanse thou me from secret faults.
Keep back thy servant also from presumptuous sins;
  let them not have dominion over me:
then shall I be upright,
  and I shall be innocent from the great transgression.
  (Ps. 19:11-13 KJV)

Our sins are so great that we can't keep track of them. We are so embroiled in them that we can't even understand them. We do not really know why we have done them nor exactly what we have done. There is no more Christian, sanctified response to the Law's just accusations than David's heartfelt prayer: "Cleanse thou me from secret faults. Keep back thy servant also from presumptuous sins." We do well to pray that every day.

Finally, the hope that is hinted at in David's request for cleansing is named in the very last verse:

Let the words of my mouth, and the meditation of my heart,
  be acceptable in thy sight,
O Lord, my strength, and my redeemer.
  (Ps. 19:14 KJV)

David could pray nothing if he did not have a redeemer. His hope is not in keeping the Law, though he certainly does want to keep the Law, but his hope is in redemption and forgiveness. And he looks for that from Yahweh Himself.

So also, the words of the Introit, the verses first quoted which extol the natural Law and the beauty of creation, are rightly understood as being Christological. They aren't just about the stars and the sun. They are also about the angels and the Messiah. The angels declare the glory of God in the firmament to shepherds in their fields. The Son of God is risen out of death, as a bridegroom coming from His chamber, and He gives life to all the earth. The creation by divine design, bearing the fingerprints of the Creator, hints at and reflects the resurrection of Jesus Christ and the redemption of the world:

> The heavens declare the glory of God;
>   and the firmament sheweth his handywork.
> Day unto day uttereth speech,
>   and night unto night sheweth knowledge.
> There is no speech nor language,
>   where their voice is not heard.
> Their line is gone out through all the earth,
>   and their words to the end of the world.
> In them hath he set a tabernacle for the sun,
>   which is as a bridegroom coming out of his chamber,
>   and rejoiceth as a strong man to run a race.
> His going forth is from the end of the heaven,
>   and his circuit unto the ends of it:
>   and there is nothing hid from the heat thereof.
>   (Ps. 19:1-6 KJV)

In ✠ *Jesus' name. Amen.*

TUESDAY OF ADVENT 4

Deuteronomy 18:15-19

In the name of the Father and of the ✠ Son and of the Holy Spirit. Amen.

After John denies that he is either the Messiah or Elijah the forerunner, the priests and Levites ask whether he is a prophet. He says that he is not. He isn't the Messiah, but he is both Elijah the forerunner and a prophet, even more than a prophet. Our Lord says so. John says that he is not Elijah because he will not take the title for himself and because they don't really know what Elijah's role in the Messianic kingdom will be, partially because they do not understand, or at least they reject, who the Messiah will be and what the Messiah will do. He doesn't want to distract them or confirm them into some superstitious confusion. So he says that he is not Elijah. In the same way, he says that he is not a prophet. That is because he is not a prophet in the way that they think of prophets. He has not come to prophesy and foretell the coming Messiah; instead, he is the voice that prepares the hearts of the people for the Lord's immediate coming by preaching repentance and comforting by the Messiah's ending of their war.

What exactly the priests and Levites are asking in John chapter 1, when they ask whether he is a prophet, is hard to pin down. The ESV translates the definite article in the question; it reads, "Are you THE prophet?" The KJV is even more explicit: "Art thou THAT prophet?" If that is the case, then the priests and Levites are asking again if John is the particular prophet foretold in Deuteronomy 18. They are asking again if he is the Messiah.

There are few problems with that. In the first place, Biblical Greek doesn't use the definite article with the same emphasis that English does. In English, we are quite emphatic with the definite article. We use it precisely. There is a big difference between "an apple" and "the apple," but in Greek the definite article is not so precise. It is often used simply to indicate a noun's case or to bring balance or formality to a clause. It is often left untranslated in English.

The second problem with this is that if they are asking John if he is the particular prophet of Deuteronomy 18, then they would be backtracking in their logic because they seem to be tracking with the actual Biblical understanding of the Messiah, the forerunner, and other prophets. What I mean is that they seem to understand that the forerunner, Elijah, is distinct from the Messiah, and not everyone did. Lots of people were confused, as it is shown when our Lord asks His disciples who people say that He is. They answer, "Some say John the Baptist, others say Elijah, and others Jeremiah or one of the prophets" (Matt. 16:14).

The priests and Levites ask first if John is the Messiah. Since he says that he isn't, they move down the list. "Well, then, are you Elijah?" When he says "no" to that, it seems strange that they would then go back and ask if he is the particular prophet of Deuteronomy 18 since that would mean that he is the Messiah. It seems more likely that they would say, "Well, if you're not the Messiah and you're not the forerunner, are you a prophet? Because we haven't had one of those in four hundred years."

The final problem is that the passage from Deuteronomy itself is hard to pin down, and it seems unlikely that the priests and Levites were viewing it as a strict and peculiar prophet. Moses tells the people that the Lord will raise up for them a prophet from their midst. He will be one of their brothers and be like him. They are to listen to him. The prophecy is repeated a couple of verses later, where it is added that the Lord Himself will put His words into this prophet's mouth and that the prophet will speak what he is commanded. Whoever will not hearken to that prophet's words will be damned.

That is certainly true of the Messiah. Our Lord Jesus Christ is a prophet like Moses from among their brethren and our brethren. He is God, yet He is a man, one of us, and He leads us out of slavery to sin.

At His baptism, which is His christening, the Father Himself speaks from heaven: "This is My beloved Son. Listen to Him." Whoever rejects the Son and His words rejects the Father and is damned.

But those things are also mostly true of Joshua, who is the immediate successor to Moses and also a type of Christ. He is not God. He is only man, but so was Moses. He comes from among the people. He speaks on God's behalf. He leads the people into the Promised Land through the Jordan on dry ground. If the people reject the Word of God through Joshua, they reject God and are damned.

So it is hard to know if Deuteronomy 18 refers only to the Messiah Himself and seems fulfilled also in Joshua and the other prophets simply because they are also types of the Messiah as Moses was, or if it is a prophecy of the continuation of the Office of the Ministry, the office of prophet, in the Old Testament, which was ultimately fulfilled in the Messiah. Most of the rabbis before Christ read the prophecy as referring to Joshua or Jeremiah or to prophets in general. None of them seems to have seen it as only referring to the Messiah.

This passage is an important one. It establishes that God will provide. Moses dies, but God's grace remains. Moses tells the people this as he is dying. Unlike Jesus, he is not coming back from the dead to preach to them again, but they will not be left alone. God is not abandoning them. Whether it refers directly to the Messiah and is merely echoed in the prophets, or whether it refers to the continuation of the office that is ultimately fulfilled in the Messiah, it demonstrates either way that God's grace, won by the Messiah, is delivered through the offices that God has established in order that His people would hear His Word and be saved. All the prophets were voices crying in the wilderness and John is the greatest, the fullest embodiment of that office. But alas, the one who is least in the kingdom of heaven is greater than he. The Lord has raised up a prophet for you in His Son. You are not abandoned or left on your own. Jesus loves you.

In ✠ Jesus' name. Amen.

WEDNESDAY OF ADVENT 4

2 Peter 3:8-14
St. Matthew 3:7-11

In the name of the Father and of the ✠ Son and of the Holy Spirit. Amen.

This scene with the Pharisees is probably why we think of John as a fiery preacher. Isaiah describes him as a comforter, but we think of him with a pointy finger and a fierce insistence that we repent.

The Pharisees were coming to be baptized by him, but rather than welcoming them as converts, he insults them: "You brood of vipers!" His rhetorical question, "Who warned you to flee from the wrath to come?" is meant to be ironic. They aren't fleeing the wrath to come. Thus he warns them, "Bear fruit in keeping with repentance, and do not presume that God will love you based upon your ancestry." In John's mouth, even the Gospel sounds threatening. "I baptize with water for repentance," he says, "but the coming one will baptize with the Holy Spirit and fire."

The problem is not in John, but in us and in the Pharisees. The tension between Law and Gospel is not in God or in His Word. Rather, it abides in the tension between our two natures: one fallen and sinful, the other redeemed and holy. Baptism with water, the Holy Spirit, and fire is all the same; it kills sinners and raises saints, and that hurts.

We don't know exactly what the problem was with the Pharisees who came to be baptized, except that they weren't truly repentant. Because of that, not only was John's baptism no good for them, but the Lord's coming in grace and mercy would be their destruction. This is hard to take for proud sinners, and it turns John's comfort into an alien work. It makes the comforter a stern and condemning figure.

Why do we balk at the offer of grace? It is because we like to think that we should have a say in things, that there ought to be some fairness, and that God should recognize our efforts. The Pharisees come to the right place, to the Jordan to be baptized by John, but for the wrong reasons. Their hearts are uncircumcised. They do not bear fruits of repentance. If you will not fall upon the stone the builders rejected and be broken, if you will not repent and insist instead upon your own way, He will fall upon you and crush you. John is not a reed bent in the wind for your amusement. He is a physician doling out the medicine of immortality to those who need it.

It isn't actually bad news, even though it sounds bad. It sounds bad because he is telling them they are dying, that they need his medicine. But it doesn't change things. It doesn't kill them; it just exposes them. They were dying whether they knew it or not, and if they will not accept his medicine, if they will not repent and trust in Christ, then they suffer not only dying but also some awareness of their dying.

And it is wonderfully good news for us, for those who have no pedigree and who have sullied ourselves with sins, for those who are dying. God, in His mercy, raises up sons for Abraham from stones, —from Gentiles and hardened sinners—and He makes them His own. He lays the axe to His own Son and spares Him not, in order that the Holy Spirit might make His home in us and bear fruit we don't even know. Here is a baptism worth having, a baptism worth dying for and worth leaving death for: a baptism of Jesus in water, Spirit, and fire.

John is not worthy to carry His sandals, and neither are we, but He washes our feet. John isn't really the Physician. Jesus is. John is the just the voice and means whereby the Physician comes to those He loves.

In ✠ Jesus' name. Amen.

Thursday of Advent 4

Philippians 4:4-7

In the name of the Father and of the ✠ Son and of the Holy Spirit. Amen.

It is one of the peculiarities of the church year, and attests to its complicated history and development, that today's Epistle is the Antiphon from last Sunday. It would seem that it should have been the Epistle last week and not today, but so it is, and it serves well to remind us that the rejoicing of the Church Militant is every bit as complicated and nuanced as its mourning. Even as we do not mourn as those without hope, neither do we rejoice as those who do not know sorrow and repentance.

Our celebration of Christmas is only a few days away. We are eager for the heavens to pour down righteousness on us through St. Mary's baby, but we also invoke today the Lord's grace to help us combat our hindering sins. The ceremonies of Advent's penitence are drawing to a close, but we still need to repent and we are still in danger. As always, that repentance and sorrow over sin is lightened by the joy that is ours in Christ. "Rejoice in the Lord always," says St. Paul, "and again, I say rejoice." For you are baptized into Christ, and He will see you through.

We need St. Paul's reminder and exhortation not so much when things are light and easy, but especially when we do not feel like rejoicing. Many people will not feel like rejoicing on Christmas, for they will sharply feel the loss of their loved ones. But they should rejoice. They rejoice in the Lord, for their loved ones who have departed with the sign of faith have not been taken from them forever, and better days are coming. Earth's joys are dim compared to what the Lord has in store for us, and we should rejoice that He has opened heaven to us in the Son.

Others might feel the terrible weight of their sins and feel ashamed on Christmas, that they have neglected the Lord's gifts or taken them lightly. We should repent, each of us, of our many sins, and we should fear the Lord and His wrath. Sins are dangerous to faith. They cause real harm to both our souls and our neighbors. We should mourn for what we've done and who we've been, and we should shake in terror at how near we've come to ruining it all.

Our sinful nature, our own fallen will and desire, along with Satan and the world, have schemed to keep us from hallowing God's name and allowing His kingdom to come to us. Our souls have been in peril. But God Himself has intervened on our behalf. He has caused us to turn and repent and receive His gracious forgiveness once again. We should not repent as those have no hope but should rather rejoice that the Lord allows us to feel our sins and not become complacent in our faith. Rejoice in the Lord always. Even in our repentance and sorrow, even when we've been brought to shame and fear, when we've felt the burden and curse of the Law, we should rejoice, for we should rejoice in the Lord always.

We should not be anxious about anything. We should repent, indeed we must repent, but we do not repent with anxiety or uncertainty. We know that God loves us in Christ. He has sent Him to atone for our sins in His self-sacrifice on the cross. He gave Himself up into death that we would not die, and He rose again as the victor so that we would live.

We know why He comes through the Virgin: to be our Savior. We know what His love for us has cost Him and that He did not count the cost too high, nor does He bear any grudge. He is the Prince of Peace coming to pour down His righteousness upon us and make us His. Rejoice! Jesus loves you. And in this be bold in everything, no matter what, by prayer and supplication with thanksgiving to let your requests be made known to God, for you are His children and He is your Father.

Thus the peace of God, which surpasses all understanding, will guard your hearts and your minds in Christ Jesus. It will not fail. Rejoice, even when you don't feel like it or want to. Rejoice in the Lord always, for it does the heart good and is always proper.

In ✠ Jesus' name. Amen.

Friday of Advent 4

James 4:17-5:7
St. John 1:15-18

In the name of the Father and of the ✠ Son and of the Holy Spirit. Amen.

John's Gospel doesn't record our Lord's birth. Instead, John starts with his famous prologue about the Word becoming flesh. It is not the Gospel for Christmas Eve. That is Luke 2: "And it came to pass in those days, that there went out a decree from Caesar Augustus that all the world should be taxed" (v. 1 KJV). John's prologue, "In the beginning was the Word, and the Word was with God, and the Word was God" (1:1 KJV), is the Gospel for Christmas Day.

That works out well for modern piety. For us, Christmas Eve is the big service. That is where the community comes. It is a time when nostalgia pulls hard at the heart strings. A few—not many, but a few—of our neighbors wander in for a glimpse of the reason for the season, for something akin to a Charlie Brown Christmas. God bless them for that! They should not be disparaged, but encouraged and prayed for. Luke 2 is the right thing for them because the first thing they need to know is the story, the details, of our Lord's suffering birth and the gift that God gave to men that they might have peace with Him.

Christmas Day is a much smaller service. Few of our neighbors come. They are busy with gifts and big meals and their own family celebrations. Those who come on Christmas Day tend to be the better catechized and more demanding of preaching and hymnody.

John's Gospel serves well because it is not meant to stand alone. It is a supplement to the other Gospels. It was written after they were and depends upon them. John's purpose is to explain, often through vivid and detailed miracles and long conversations, what the others showed. He doesn't go into the whole Bethlehem bit because he expects you to already know it. As such, his Gospel is the most theological, and most our favorite passages are from it.

Here then is John's explanation of Luke 2, of what it meant that Jesus was born in Bethlehem: "For from his fullness we have all received, grace upon grace. For the law was given through Moses; grace and truth came through Jesus Christ."

God has come into the world through the Virgin, taken up our flesh and our cause, made Himself a man to be sacrificed in our place, to pour grace upon us. John gives us a hint as to what the character of that grace is: it is grace upon grace. John shows us this when Jesus makes water into wine and gives them not only the best wine but more wine than they could drink. Grace upon grace, extravagant, wasteful. He shows us this again as Jesus multiplies the loaves and there is too much left over, when the miraculous catch of fish is too big to haul in, when He saves and forgives the woman caught in adultery, and in many other instances. But, of course, the clearest showing of the extravagant, even reckless, grace of God in Jesus Christ is when He is lifted up from the earth and draws us to Himself. Grace upon grace, bestowed on those who don't deserve it, who could have never earned it or found it or figured it out. Grace undeserved, unexpected, upon grace: glorious, free, and perfect forgiving love.

That is why Jesus was born, why He came into the world, in this truth, for the sake of grace. Grace upon grace: that is how it is with the Lord.

In ☩ Jesus' name. Amen.

CHRISTMAS VIGIL—MORNING

Isaiah 7:10-14
Romans 1:1-6
St. Matthew 1:18-25

In the name of the Father and of the ✠ Son and of the Holy Spirit. Amen.

St. Joseph showed himself to be a godly and wise man. He had no hubris, no excess. Even though he had been wronged and had the right, he would not shame St. Mary. He was set to suffer the loss of his betrothed, to put her away quietly and suffer her shame in himself.

The philosophers would have approved. This was the best and wisest, the most decent and ideal course; no good comes from vengeance or making a scene. But an angel intervened. The child came by the Holy Spirit, not by a man. Mary's virginity, her loyalty, and her love for Joseph remained pure. It was not merely lip service; it was real. And things were not quite what they seemed. This child is the Lord who saves His people. He is the Messiah.

Now if Joseph took the first news well and planned to act in an honorable way, then this news was that much tougher. For even then Joseph could have acted out his part; he could have put her away quietly and no one could have blamed him, not even God. Indeed, he still would have been counted as a decent and honorable man. The angel did not tell him that he had to take Mary as his wife. He was only told that he should not be afraid to take her. Whatever the wagging tongues of Nazareth were saying, she had not been unfaithful.

Reality rarely stops gossip. Joseph knew then that the gossip wasn't true, but his shame, even though it was undeserved, remained. Even if the wagging tongues heard the truth, they were unlikely to believe it. And if they did believe it, gossips are always liars. They embellish their tales even when they know that it is false. That is the first point: Joseph is going to be shamed no matter what.

Next, despite the fact that Mary was faithful, what can't be denied is that God took Mary from Joseph. He impregnated her. It could well be that Joseph would never be allowed to consummate the marriage or have any children by Mary. In any case, Mary had been taken from him. Joseph would never be her first or deepest love. Again, he was legally and morally free to walk away and simply know in his heart that she hadn't betrayed him, that she and he were both honorable no matter how it appeared. That is the second point: Even as there is no escape from shame, so also there is no escape from the cross. God is to blame.

But Joseph had wisdom, not just beyond caring about the opinions of men, but also beyond that of Aristotle. True wisdom, that which begins with the fear of the Lord, occasionally directs us to do things that the wise of this world label as foolish, impractical, and extreme, like dying rather than pretending to pray to Caesar or taking a wife pregnant with someone else's child. Joseph submitted to God's will. He clung to the tenacious hope that God is good. Of his own will, he took up the guardianship of both Mary and the Messiah. In doing so, he took up a cross like few men have ever known, and the dirty minds and petty men of this world snickered at him and his bride all of their days. They called the Son of God a bastard. When Joseph went to Bethlehem for the census, there was no room for his family in the homes of his family members and friends who lived in Bethlehem. From there he was forced into exile in Egypt.

And if James and these others were sons from a previous marriage, as tradition has it, what must they have thought? Their father had gone mad in his old age, marrying a young girl and taking on the child of another. And what did they think of that child who seemed never to do any wrong; who was ever obedient, generous, and kind; who made them look bad; and who caused and required such great sacrifice and expense for all who came near unto Him? He may have loved His neighbor as Himself, been the perfect son and brother, but His presence is always dangerous and always brings suffering. It was not Mary's heart alone that was pierced, then or now.

That is the cost of wisdom and the reason that it is so uncommon. Men on their own cannot obtain it. When they glimpse it, they think it foolish. Not even Socrates, Plato, or Aristotle could boast of the wisdom and self-control of simple Joseph, for he was a man who knew himself and his limitations, a man of moderation and decency. But above all, he was a man who trusted that God works all things together for good and that God would provide. He knew the mercy that endures forever, that joins itself to the flesh of men to be a sacrifice for sin and a beacon of light and life in this dark and dying world. Joseph knew what it was to belong to someone else and to trust in His goodness and providence. Thus writes Solomon: "The fear of the LORD is the beginning of wisdom" (Ps. 111:10).

We would be remiss, however, if we did not mention the other extreme virtue in Joseph. We'd call it *romance*; the ancients called it *love*. Joseph didn't act merely for the sake of honor or for what was wise. No doubt, what really scared Joseph was not the possibility, seemingly evident, of Mary's moral weakness but the idea that she did not love him, did not want him. He thought he had lost her, probably to some young, good-looking man, and that he could not compete. He was broken-hearted, but he would not stand in the way of her happiness. He would quietly end the engagement so that she could move on, even if he was unable to.

In Joseph, we see not merely honor but also a willingness to sacrifice, born of love. Joseph loved Mary. When the angel told him, "Do not be afraid to take Mary as your wife, for the child in her womb was conceived by the Holy Spirit," he was freed. This meant she had not been unfaithful; she still loved him. He could still have her. And Joseph loved Jesus also. An adopted son is no less a son, in any way at all, than a biological son.

So don't feel too sorry for him. He got what he wanted. He got to marry and live with Mary until he died. He got to guard and protect, love and serve, provide for and wait upon her and upon Jesus for the rest of his life. Thus was he willing to take up that cross and be the Lord's guardian. He counted her worthy of the cost, even as God so counted him.

In this way, the Lord provided a father and guardian for Mary and for her baby, that this baby might go forth for the love of evil men like us and buy us out of captivity with His death and pour His life into us through His resurrection, that the Holy Spirit would also overshadow us.

Joseph was exactly right: the Lord works all things together for good. Merry Christmas.

In ✠ Jesus' name. Amen.

CHRISTMAS MIDNIGHT

Isaiah 9:2-7
Titus 2:11-14
St. Luke 2:1-20

In the name of the Father and of the ✠ *Son and of the Holy Spirit. Amen.*

Imagine Bethlehem the night our Lord was born. God is there. He is recognized by ox and donkey, praised by angelic choirs. The stars adjust themselves to look down. It looks like heaven.

Don't be fooled. Salvation is not in heaven. It is on earth, where the Savior was born for us earthlings. Heaven is not some distant place. It is here, on earth. Do not think that you must ascend to God, that you must conquer heaven by violence or works, sneak in, or charm the Lord. Unto you is born a Savior, on earth, here. He has descended. He has leaped down from heaven.

I behold a new and wondrous mystery! My ears resound to the shepherd's song. The angels sing. My heart is stirred. A Savior is born—unto me!—in Bethlehem, on earth. The archangels blend their voices in harmony. The cherubim resound their joyful praise. The seraphim exalt His glory.

But the Savior is not born unto them, to angels and archangels, in heaven. He does not come to save angels. He is born—unto me!—on earth, a Savior.

And unto you. He is born unto all of you, to shepherds and priests, bankers and police, soldiers and salesmen. He is born unto the good and bad, frequent attenders and once-a-year-stoppers-by, to the faithful and not-so-faithful. A Savior is born unto you and He is no respecter of persons. He does not check pedigrees or attendance records. He is not impressed by the person who gives generously. He is not offended by the one who gives nothing. He is born unto all. He is born unto you.

This is the cause of our holy feast. It is holy food for holy people, that is, for you. Do not think you are not holy. You are holy for the Lord God has declared you holy in His Son. The feast this night is nothing less than His body and blood given in bread and wine. God has a body. God has blood. God has a soul. God is a man, born unto us, that the hearts of men might be glad and free of sin and come back to their Creator without shame or terror, but in joy.

The Savior is born unto you in Bethlehem, the house of bread, on earth. It is no coincidence that He lacked a crib and was placed instead into a feeding trough. He was born unto you to be bread: bread for beasts, bread for wolves, and bread for sheep. He comes in His body to feed you into life, to slake your thirst, to satisfy your soul. He is put into a manger, not only because He is rejected by men and there is no room for Him in Bethlehem's inns but also because He gives Himself to you, as food, on earth.

And if this great cosmic event causes angels to sing for joy, how much more should you, unto whom the Savior is born, sing and praise God's holy name? The shepherds come to gather sheep. So follow them. Be gathered. Rejoice and be glad. Behold the Godhead on earth, in the manger, wrapping Himself in your sins as a man, subjecting Himself to your death. He is born unto you, a Savior.

Do not ask how it is accomplished. Do not ask how God can be in the manger and in heaven at the same time, how He can be God and man. You might as well ask how God can be in heaven and be present on all the Christian altars of the world in His body and His blood. Where God wills, the order of nature is overturned. It is His nature, His creation, and He turns it as He pleases.

What we call science is but a feeble attempt to discern the laws and rules we can observe. It is most useful and is blessed by God, but there are things we cannot observe and there are things we mistake. In Christ, the finite holds the infinite: God is a man, not as we observe, but as He promises. So also do we fail to comprehend or observe how it is that He is Alpha and Omega, without beginning and without end.

This is His will, His promise, and His grace. He is God. He is man. He is born unto you and He is your Savior. He had the power and the right. He descended. He took up your flesh to make Himself a sacrifice on your behalf. Then He humbled Himself, denied Himself the full and constant use of His divine rights and powers—for a time, as a man—so that He might suffer in your place and die. All things move in obedience to the Lord. Even thorns, nails, and spears move in obedience to the Lord. So also do census takers, Roman crosses, and even virgin wombs. It is His will to be born unto you, to be your Savior on earth. He wills to take up flesh, to be God and man at the same time without compromising either, so it is. A Savior is born. Humanity is rescued. Hell is undone. You receive a reward you did not earn and reap where you did not sow.

You are more blessed than the holy angels. You have more cause to sing. Least in the kingdom of God, you are greater even than John the unbending Baptist.

That heavenly scene in Bethlehem will not last. The angels only sing there once. The ox and donkey go back to ox and donkey ways. And then things turn quite hellish for Bethlehem. The satan Herod vents his rage toward the little town. Christ the Lord, the Savior, is exiled and chased about the earth until hell moves its focus to Galilee, and then to Jerusalem, driving pigs off cliffs, sowing betrayal into the hearts of friends, and crucifying the Son of God, on earth. The city of peace becomes the city of injustice and idolatry.

But the Savior will not shrink from His course on earth. He is not afraid, nor is He hesitant. He was born unto you for this. They do not take His life from Him; He lays it down to have you. He was born unto you for this. And out of the grave He will spring back to life, a man, body and soul, the second person of the Godhead, the Deity, the Savior, who was born unto you, alive out of death, to redeem and save you on earth.

Unto you is born this day in the city of David a Savior, which is Christ the Lord.

This is all our hope, all our life, and our salvation. Thus do we sing with angelic joy: "Glory be to God on high and on earth peace, good will toward men." Jesus is born and Jesus lives.†

In ✠ Jesus' name. Amen.

---

† With some help from the "Homily on the Nativity of the Lord" by St. John Chrysostom, http://www.abbamoses.com/stjohnnativity.html (accessed 9/9/14).

CHRISTMAS DAY

Exodus 40:17-21, 34-38
Hebrews 1:1-6
St. John 1:1-18

In the name of the Father and of the ✠ Son and of the Holy Spirit. Amen.

The birth of Jesus Christ not only shows the redemption of creation but also affirms the goodness of creation. Some of what was good was lost when Adam took that lustful bite and plunged the world back to chaos, but it was not all lost. Apples bruise and get eaten by worms or disease, but they still taste sweet and they still provide vitamins and sustenance and even blossoms in the spring. All of creation, even apples, groans under the strain that we have put upon it by our sins. It longs for the revelation of the sons of God. But still there is goodness in creation: kittens and sugarplums, iPods and cranberries. Creation was and still is the object of God's love, created by His Word, and that is good.

God loves His creation. Thus He made an immediate promise upon Adam's fall: Satan would not win. He could not have them. He could not have the apples or any of the stuff, and, most significantly, he could not have Adam, Eve, or their offspring. Save one, but we'll get to that in a bit. What God has made belongs to Him. Satan tried to steal it, but he cannot have it. The Lord takes it back.

Still, the Lord is just. He will not steal back what was stolen. He will pay a fair price, even if it was ill-gotten gain for hell. And there is one offspring of Eve, an impossibly uncreated seed, a man born without the will of man and without Adam's sin, who is handed over. He is the ransom and the scapegoat. He is the victim and the priest. He is the Son of Mary and the Son of His Father Almighty. He will give up His life to gain back the deceived and stolen souls of men. But in the act, He will crush the serpent's head, who bites off more than he can chew and is undone.

Adam and Eve had wanted, in their greed, to become like God. So God became like them, was incarnate, was made man: the Word became flesh. Thus did the Lord make them, and us, more fully human. It also made them, and us, more fully His sons and His daughters. He promoted them, and us, beyond Eden to heaven itself. He makes new heavens and a new earth.

Now some might ask, "If God is so in love with the earth and if He promises 'peace on earth' at the Savior's birth, where is it? Where is the peace?" It is there in the manger: God in the flesh, the Prince of Peace subject to Satan's tyranny. God the Father, the Son, and the Holy Spirit is the perfect lover. He does not force Himself upon the earth. He will take back all the apples and gerbils, sharks and trees, but He will not take back by force any person who does not want Him. He loves you so you are free. If you do not want Him, if you want to go where there is perfect equality, no hierarchy, no dependence on another, no sacrifice; if you want to be where things are fair and to be alone, you may go and join the devil in his domain. The Lord is a lover, not a rapist. He has made you and He has bought you, but you are not a slave. You are a bride. He was sold for the price of a slave, but He doesn't buy you as one. His purchase was not your price, but your ransom. He would have you love Him and rejoice in Him, so He leaves you free.

It is that freedom that allows humanity to engage in all sorts of evil. Nations wage war, men fornicate and commit adultery, liars tell lies, and the economy crumbles because God loves the world and will not force Himself upon it. He does not win the world by violence. He loves it and redeems it by suffering violence. He does not force you away from your stuff or your sins, even from the devil. Instead, He joins you in your sorrow. He is Emmanuel, God with us. He comes not simply to show you a better way—like unto Ghandi or Mother Teresa, though He certainly does show you a better way, a fuller and more satisfying life, wisdom—but more than that, more than showing a way, He comes to actually to bear your burden, to suffer the consequences of your sins, to defeat death on your behalf. He wins you back by sacrifice and you are free. He is wooing you. He is loving you.

That is the peace He brings. That is peace by which He rules. It is peace between Himself and us rebels. It is the end of war with heaven. Some might think it is not quite good enough or what it could be. They want peace here and now. They want the Lord to end all sorrow instantaneously or at least end it for those who love Him, like unto the perverted fantasies of Timothy LaHaye where the believers get to check out of creation for being good. But our Lord does not do that. That is because the Lord does not love you alone. He does not only love the believers or good people. He loves all the world. To love Him back is to also love what He loves, to love apples and snowbanks and mountains and eagles; Afghans, Iraqis, Germans, and Poles; good and bad, greatest and least. He didn't give up on you. He is not giving up on them. He did not force you. He will not force them. And He gives you a part in this love, in His kingdom, by giving you duties and services to perform for those whom He loves, even giving you crosses to bear.

His love is not shallow, so He does not keep you from sorrow. Compassion is born of sorrow, and freedom always suffers abuse. If the Lord put an end to all hunger, he would also deny you the joy of feeding those you love and those in need. And without hunger, there also would be no feasting.

The Lord leaves you free. He suffers the consequences and inevitable abuse. He leaves you free because He loves you. He waits and He loves. You are worth it to Him. You are worth the risk, the pain, the disappointment, and the sorrow. For like a woman just delivered, He forgets the agony for the joy set before Him. He delights in you. Listen and you'll hear Him say in the delivery room, "Open your eyes so that I can see you."

That is what mothers of newborns frequently say when they can see all of their babies except for the eyeballs. Why is that they want so badly to look into their newborn's eyes? Because they want to know their children. It is not a stretch to imagine St. Mary holding our Lord in her arms and saying, "Open your eyes so that I can see you."

That is very much the sentiment of our Lord who says to us, "Ask and it shall be given unto you." It is like a mother's desire to look into her child's eyes. He wants to know you. That is why He loves your prayers. You are free and unique. Your prayers are different from everyone else's, even as your story is different and wonderful. You delight Him. He adores you and wants to look into your eyes, to know you.

Still there is more. The Lord loves creation. He has redeemed it that you, like Him, would have someone to love. It is not just that you receive love. He has also redeemed you as a lover. You love people and stuff around you. St. Francis was on to something with his talk of "brother bird." The Lord redeemed creation even as He created it. He has made it lovable. But even more so, the Lord redeemed humanity, the Word became flesh, so that you might look across the aisle or across the ocean and see not enemies or foreigners, but brothers and sisters. He places the solitary into families. He took up flesh to love you, that you would love one another. That love is not shallow or cheap. Children always break your heart. But if they didn't, what good would they be?

He is still Emmanuel, still God with us. He is still a man. And He still loves creation and loves you. But He is no longer in the manger. He has grown and died, risen and ascended, yet He is not gone. He is here on the earth, in creation, in bread and wine, in water and Word, in brother and in sister, shining in the darkness, not just to redeem but also to affirm. For He has made and declared them good. This is the peace that passes all understanding.

He has come unto His own. He has come to you. By grace you receive Him. You are His child. God be praised, evermore and evermore.

In ✠ Jesus' name. Amen.

The Second Day of Christmas
St. Stephen, Protomartyr

December 26

2 Chronicles 24:17-22
Acts 6:8-7:2, 51-60
St. Matthew 23:34-39

In the name of the Father and of the ✠ Son and of the Holy Spirit. Amen.

Stephen stands before that hateful, violent mob without fear. What can they do to him? They can't kill him. God is on his side, has given His life for his, has promised him eternal glory in the Father's presence. If it is his time, if his suffering witness is complete, then God will bring him home, but not a moment before.

Stephen sees clearly through the dross. The Lord has lovingly disciplined him so that he would not mistake this fallen creation, success, popularity, or an abundance of things for what God actually desires to give to him. Stephen's expectations about this life are realistic because they come from the Scriptures. He knows that men always resist the Holy Spirit and do evil. He knows also that God is still good and still loves men, and the sacrifice of His Son on the cross is enough to forgive even scheming, diabolical murderers. Again and again, men reject God. Again and again, He reaches out to them with grace, forgiveness, and peace.

Do not miss the profound effect of Stephen's dying prayer: Saul is no longer at odds with Stephen. They are brothers in heaven, fellow martyrs of Christ who have come to their reward. Stephen's prayer was answered. Paul was saved by grace and reconciled to the one he murdered. God is good.

Dry turkey, missing batteries, and family squabbles still hurt. So do stones. But they will not last. They will not hurt forever. Your time, too, will come. And there are no disappointments in your true home. Jesus was born, died, and rose that He would bring you there. Here is the answer to your disappointments, the answer to your sin, and the answer to death. The Lord desires to gather you to Himself no less than He desired to gather Jerusalem.

Come and eat. The babe of Bethlehem, alive out of the grave, is here for you.

In ✠ *Jesus' name. Amen.*

The Third Day of Christmas
St. John, Apostle and Evangelist

December 27

Revelation 1:1-6
1 John 1:1-10
St. John 21:20-25

In the name of the Father and of the ✠ Son and of the Holy Spirit. Amen.

The love of God toward us was manifested, was shown, in God sending his only begotten Son into the world. The Virgin was overshadowed by the Holy Spirit. She gave birth to a Son. He is God and man, God with us and for us, as one of us. He is the one by whom all things were made. He became flesh—was made, created, in Mary's womb, our brother—and dwelt among us to purify, cleanse, and reclaim us, to love us. He is life, love, and light.

He has loved us by laying down His life, by being overcome by darkness, by being a guilt-offering for our sin. And in Him, we—who have been baptized into Him, who by grace confess not just our sin but also Him, who have been cleansed by His blood—are alive. In Him, we are the beloved of the Father and of the Son and of the Spirit. In Him, we have fellowship. We live in the light, by and for and in that most Holy Trinity.

That is John's message. It is the message of Christmas and Easter as well. It is the message of the Early Church and the Medieval Church and of the Reformation. It is the message of all the apostles, prophets, and martyrs. It is proclaimed to you that you also would have this fellowship, this holy communion with the Father and the Son in the Spirit. In that holy fellowship you are united also to John, to Peter and Paul, and to one another. Communion means *at one with*. You are one with Christ and, in Him, are at one with one another and all the saints.

This is impossible love, this holy reconciliation and fellowship. It changes everything. It turns brawny, unruly fisherman into preachers and missionaries, martyrs and prophets. It dissolves ethnic barriers, distinctions of class and sex. In Christ there is neither Jew nor Greek, male nor female. It removes not just the eternal consequence of sin, but sin itself. It turns erstwhile sinners into saints. It even gives them good works to perform for the benefit of their neighbors. It makes them God's voice and God's hands on earth.

God became man to be your brother. The Father rejected the Son on the cross in order to adopt you into His household. The Holy Spirit has made your heart His temple and your mouth His witness.

And if that weren't enough, He bids you come, bask in His grace, hear His life-giving, life-changing words. Feast upon the bread of life that bestows and sustains life: His risen body. Be joined again to Him. Be in communion with Him and with one another, at one in will and doctrine, for the Word made flesh makes common bread into that same flesh, the Word embodied. He places Himself, body and blood, God and man, into your frail body for your eternal good that you would be like Him. Thus your eyes see the Word of Life, and you rejoice with Simeon. Your hands, or at least your tongues, touch Him. What John has written makes your joy full and eternal.

In ✠ Jesus' name. Amen.

The Fourth Day of Christmas
Holy Innocents

December 28

Jeremiah 31:15-17
Revelation 14:1-5
St. Matthew 2:13-18

In the name of the Father and of the ☩ Son and of the Holy Spirit. Amen.

He came unto His own. His own received Him not. It is not merely wicked Herod. It is all of Jerusalem that rejects Him, for all of Jerusalem is deeply troubled at the coming of the wise men from the East.

The wise men want to know where the King of kings, the Prince of Peace, is to be born. They are wise by virtue of Daniel. He had prophesied in their country. He must have brought them at least some of the books of Moses, for they have Balaam's promised sign of a star. They have seen it fulfilled. By faith, with trust that the God of Moses has fulfilled these things and provided a Savior, they come to worship the one thereby announced. But the star, for the time being, has only led them to Jerusalem, and they do not know where the Messiah is.

It seems that they did not have all of the Old Testament, that they did not have even all of the things written by the time of Daniel. In any case, they did not have Micah's promise to Bethlehem, even though Micah predates Daniel. But it was not a great mystery as to where the Messiah was to be born for those who did. The priests were well-trained in the Scriptures. They knew all about the thirty pieces of silver and the potter's field. They were quick to respond to the wise inquiry: "Bethlehem."

And yet, none of those Biblical scholars followed the wise men to Bethlehem. Instead, they were troubled with Herod, and all Jerusalem with them. They were not rejoicing. They were raging, plotting. They did not want the Messiah and the necessary upset that He would bring to the world. Herod lashed out with Satanic hatred and violence unequaled in all of time, and he did so with the consent of both Jerusalem and the theologians. The boys of Bethlehem and their mothers bore the brunt of that wicked rage.

The boys gave up their lives while the fullness of God hidden in Mary's babe slipped off in the night. What kind of a God is this who lets the babies die? What kind of a reward is this for David's city? Where is the peace pronounced by angels to the shepherds in Bethlehem's fields? Where is God's good will toward men?

The answer is not very satisfying to our intellect: the ways of God are not our ways. His thoughts are not our thoughts. But it is satisfying to faith. And if you think that you have plumbed those depths, that you understand Him, that His ways and thoughts make sense, then you have committed idolatry. You are worshiping a figment of your imagination which you call God but who looks and thinks like you. Repent. He is not fully comprehensible and we cannot judge Him. We have no right to make demands or to insist on what seems just to us. We submit in faith and wait for His goodness to be revealed.

What we have is what He has given us. We have His Word. It is His revelation to us, His self-revealing. We can go nowhere else. In that Holy Book we are told that in this way, by the horror of Herod's slaughter in Bethlehem, is the prophecy from Hosea fulfilled: "[O]ut of Egypt I called my son" (Hos. 11:1). That was the purpose and it is good. The boys died. Their mothers mourned and refused comfort. Jesus escaped in weakness, and in weakness He came forth again from Egypt after Herod's death. He is the Lamb led to the slaughter without complaint or resistance, but not until the appointed time. He responded to Herod's violence, even as He would later to Caiaphas and Pilate, with humility.

He submitted to their violence, but only of His own will, in His own time, on His own terms. God is hidden in the weakness of that infant flesh. No one forces His hand. The daring rescue of mankind that will cost Him His life cannot be thwarted, but it will only be accomplished when all things are fulfilled. In the meantime, the boys of Bethlehem are spared a life of suffering. They went early to their reward. Unlike their mothers, their hearts were never broken. They were never lonely. And thanks be to God, they never had to suffer the disabling sadness that comes from outliving one's children.

They died that day so that Jesus might escape and return to die for them. His martyrdom is the liberating gift to the boys of Bethlehem. His life is exchanged for theirs. They seemed to die that day, but they really lived. Herod delivered them to heaven, peace, and joy without measure. Thus they praise God still, not by speaking but by dying. Their lives are empty of themselves and are filled with Him.

So it must be for each of us. The life Jesus lived, He lived for us. The death He died, He died for us. And the resurrection to which He rose, He rose for us. When we are broken upon Him, who was rejected by the appointed builders but made the chief stone by the Father in heaven, then the life, death, and resurrection of Jesus is ours. He breaks us, empties us, so that He might rebuild and fill us. He slays us so that He might raise us again to life. His ways are not our ways: they are better, even when they hurt. In the end, we are the ones who are called out of Egypt and away from Pharaoh's slavery to sin and death. He makes us weak, like children, and then in Him—only in Him, always in Him—we are strong.

"He came unto his own, and his own received him not. But as many as received him, to them gave he power to become the sons of God, even to them that believe on his name" (John 1:11-12 KJV). The boys of Bethlehem were not abandoned. Their mothers found comfort in the wounds of Jesus who died also for them. Now they have been reunited with their sons. They will never be separated again. And already now, after maybe fifty long years of grief here on earth without their babies, they have enjoyed nearly two thousand years in perfect bliss won by Jesus with their children. Thus saith the Lord to the women of Ramah who refused comfort, "Refrain thy voice from weeping, and thine eyes from tears: for thy work shall be rewarded, saith the LORD; and [thy children] shall come again from the land of the enemy" (Jer. 31:16 KJV). Death is not the end. The enemy loses. He does not get our children. He does not get us. Rachel is rewarded.

Thus St. Paul writes: "For I reckon that the sufferings of this present time are not worthy to be compared with the glory which shall be revealed in us" (Rom. 8:18 KJV).

God be praised. He does all things well.

In ✠ Jesus' name. Amen.

THE FIFTH DAY OF CHRISTMAS

December 29

Isaiah 9:2-7
Titus 2:11-14
St. Luke 2:1-14

In the name of the Father and of the ☩ Son and of the Holy Spirit. Amen.

When the fullness of time had come, when our Lord was to be born into our flesh, Caesar decreed that the whole world be enrolled, counted, and listed, so that he might get his due. What Caesar could never know was that this served more than getting our Lord to the house of bread on time. It also served that He might be openly declared to the Gentiles, that He Himself would be counted and listed, as a man, one of us, in the flesh, even owing taxes to Caesar.

It may be surprising, but the Lord who has submitted to Caesar's census has a census of His own. He enrolls His elect. He counts and lists them by name in the book of life as they are baptized into His death and resurrection.

What Caesar unknowingly orchestrated, Micah foretold. The Lord is born in Bethlehem, the ancestral town of David whose name means *house of bread*. The Messiah born there is the living bread who came down from heaven. He gives Himself as a man, in a feeding trough, archaically called a manger, that He would be food for men, those beasts who sought to steal from God the gifts He gladly gives. He has come down from heaven, driven to Bethlehem by Caesar's lust for bread, to be the bread by which men might live.

No, men don't live by bread alone. Men live by every word that proceeds from the mouth of God. But this Word in Bethlehem, this bread, proceeds from the Father and the Spirit. He has become the bread of life for men. By this bread alone do men actually live and not by any other word. Only this Word is from the mouth of God, so only this bread gives life.

Thus He is born in Bethlehem, the house of bread. He is the Word made flesh in the midst of a census. And now the sons of Adam eat their way out of the curse even as they had eaten their way into it. The Lord is bread for men, and in bread His body is given for the forgiveness of sins and the end of war.

He was born out of doors. There was no fox's hole or bird's nest for Him. In Bethlehem all He gets is a borrowed cave or stable, if that, and a pile of straw or hay in the cold, dark night. He came into this world already on a journey, away from home, driven by power-hungry politicians, and He is already rejected by His relatives in Bethlehem, the house of selfish, moldy bread.

Those who follow Him are likewise sojourners. This place is not our home. We travel on the way that He has gone, for He is the way. We travel through the cross and grave, back to the Father. It is a painful journey full of temptation and sin, out of sync with Caesar, out of sync with Bethlehem, subjected to the scorn of the world, but accompanied by angels.

That is why you aren't satisfied here. Christmas, as glorious as it might be, is never quite what we think it should be, could be, or ought to be. That is because we are on a journey. Babies don't belong in stables and we don't belong here. We belong to the Father. He has claimed us through His Son's blood, blood that is poured down our throats to purify our selfish, moldy hearts and make us His. We journey back to Him, and our hearts are restless until they find rest in Him.

This is why an angel appears to the watching shepherds and the brightness of God shone round about them. This shows us that the Lord reveals Himself not to Caesar, but to the lowly, and that His people are sheep. That is an insult in our day, but it is an honor in the kingdom of

God. The sheep are cared for by shepherds—pastors, in Latin. Those pastors are to announce what the angels have sung: peace on earth.

There is an epic backstory to this angelic son. There was a war in heaven. Satan was cast down. He came to earth. He recruited us in the garden, willing accomplices and traitors. We chose to join up with him, against God. We rebelled and announced our proud hatred of God with selfish, moldy hearts.

But God would not let it be. He would not let us be. He is an active creator. He was not done with us, His creatures. He walked in the garden. He came to us in our shame and sin. He cursed Satan: "I will put enmity between you and the woman, and between your [seed] and her [seed]; he shall bruise your head, and you shall bruise his heel" (Gen. 3:15).

God would not let us be. He would not leave us on Satan's side. He put enmity between us. That means that He made us and the devil to be enemies. That enmity—that which stands between us and the devil, the source of our being enemies—is the seed of the Virgin Eve, born without impotent Adam, but by the overshadowing of the Holy Spirit. He, Enmity, stands between us and the devil.

Fallen men may reject God. They may hate Him. But they will also hate, and be hated by, Satan. Enmity stands between us and the devil. He will never be our ally or friend or comrade. Even if fallen men reject God and choose to be on Satan's side, God chooses nonetheless to be on their side, on our side.

That is what He has done. He sent His seed, born of the Virgin. He took up our cause, our side, against Satan in the terrible war that Satan began. Satan bruised His heel to death, drained Him of His life on the cross. But He, the Lord, the bread for men, was vindicated by His Father. He was raised again from the dead. He has crushed Satan once and for all, for us, in our place, as our hero and captain and redeemer.

He will not let Satan win. He bears the cost of our rebellion and ransom in His own body, once laid in a manger, once received not by His own. He gives His life for yours. That is the sum of it, the Gospel of angels to shepherds: a Savior, a substitute, is born.

That is the peace that the angels are singing about. The war in heaven came to earth. Our sin, our joining with Satan, caused discord and strife between heaven and earth. It distanced us from our holy cousins, the angels. It made us their enemies. But God has become flesh, has been born in Bethlehem, the house of bread, to make us His, to reconcile us to the Father. And in that reconciliation, in that bread, we are reconciled also again to the holy angels.

That is why Jesus was born, why God walked in the garden, why He still speaks in His Word. This is what gives us joy in the midst of this sad and uncertain journey, in the dark and cold of winter, in the sadness of the cemetery. Jesus was born at night, shining in the darkness, and the darkness cannot seize Him. Therefore it cannot seize us.

We are enrolled in the census of heaven by the waters of Holy Baptism. We belong to God. We eat His body. We drink His blood. His name is upon us. But we owe Him no taxes. He is for us, and we are not His slaves, but His bride. Thus we have peace with Him and with the holy angels and with the whole company of heaven.

And that is what makes for a most Merry Christmas, twelve days long and into eternity.†

In ✠ Jesus' name. Amen.

---

† Inspired by and borrowed from a sermon by Gregory the Great, posted at *Gottesdienst Online* on 12/11/12, http://gottesdienstonline.blogspot.com/2012/12/christmas-eve-help-//from-st-gregory-great.html.

The Sixth Day of Christmas

December 30

Exodus 40:17-21, 34-38
Titus 3:4-7
St. John 1:1-14

In the name of the Father and of the ✠ Son and of the Holy Spirit. Amen.

Nothing can ruin Christmas. Not sticks, not stones, not broken bones. Not lies or false names, nor cruel words, nor even divorce. Not war. Not hunger. Not drunkenness, nor neglect. Not old grudges. Not fresh wounds. Not bad news from doctors, teachers, or the stock market. None of that. And if none of that, then certainly not dry turkey or boring presents or disgruntled children and boorish guests.

Nothing can ruin Christmas. Not even death. For death has lost its sting, the grave its victory. Death has been put to rest in the manger. It dares not rear its fallen head. For if the ox and the donkey know their master, how much more does death know who has caused its demise? Christmas cannot be ruined anymore than God can be ruined or the birth in Bethlehem undone. The Word became flesh. That is a fact that endures. Christmas is not over. It does not end. We have a Savior, and this fallen realm is not our home.

God as a man, God as a baby, has laid Himself into the manger to make Himself food for men made beasts by inwardness and selfish lust. He is the bread of life. He gives Himself to palates dulled by evil words, to men already drunk who don't appreciate Him. Their failures and wickedness will not stop Him. He will do what He was sent to do despite our greedy sins. He will make men His.

He enters into our house of death. His light shines and drives off the darkness. Sins dissolve like cobwebs before the sun, like fog melting away on a hot August day. God loves you. He gives Himself to men that men might then give themselves to Him and that, in that exchange, men would be whole, free and clean and full of praise, zealous for good works and service to neighbors.

He has redeemed us. He has rescued us out of death, out of gloom and despair. And though we still mourn, though we still weep and know some touch of anger and frustration, we do not mourn as those who have no hope. We know the truth: the Word became flesh. We've seen the light on sacred page and heard it in sacred song. We've felt the watery hand of God and His name is upon us. We are His.

The Word became flesh. Our frail flesh will soon leave behind the corruption of this present age and be like the angels in heaven—holy, alive and good, full of pious mirth—because the Word became flesh and now flesh endures. God as man was laid to rest once in a manger. So also was He laid into a borrowed tomb. But no more. He is not a baby and He is not dead. That flesh sits at the right hand of the Father. That flesh does not rot or turn to dust. That flesh endures. And that flesh ushers in all believers, pointing to the blessed, enduring marks on His hands and feet and side, advocating, mediating, shepherding men through death and into life, out of dust and into endurance. The Word became flesh and the Word endures forever. Thus corruptible becomes incorruptible and the mortals become immortal, and we are saved.

This will abide. It will last. No one can snatch the Word made flesh from us. Long after the glitter and schmaltz and the crowds at the mall are gone, the Word they still shall let remain. They may not care for it. They may hate it. But it matters not, for it is the Word that none can deny nor mistake. He endures forever.

He is that blessed Word that came from God to save our race. He is that blessed Word that created all that is, that blessed Word which was sent from God to speak us back into fellowship with Him. He is not done. He endures and so shall we and so too will our festivities.

The last word has not yet been said. The waters of Holy Baptism still wash over His people. The Word of grace still comes from His ministers and absolves the penitents who seek His grace. His Word still calls bread and wine to be flesh for food of life, and that flesh—once laid into a manger and nailed to a cross, made alive out of death again—is still laid upon the tongues of men and makes them temples of the Holy Spirit. His Word does what it was sent to do. He calls us back. He speaks us clean. He forgives our sins and gives us faith and gives us eternity.

He cannot be stopped. Still, He is not done. The Word is cast, the Word made flesh, and enters into the hearts of men by way of the ear and the mouth and the skin and declares them good. He gives us Himself and joins Himself to men, that they might be joined to Him. He brings them by the Spirit to the Father, as a bride immaculate and pure, purchased and won with the blood of God's flesh out of the Virgin's womb. This is a marriage that lasts forever.

Did His own receive Him not? Was there no room for Him in the inn? It did not stop Him. He still loves men. He took our flesh. He redeemed our race from this awful, dying place. He has laid Himself not only into a manger surrounded by dung in the cold winter air but also onto the rough wood of a cross surrounded by liars and cheats, thieves and terrorists. He has loved us to the very end. No price was too great, not even the life of His Son made man. That love, that willing sacrifice, endures and lasts.

There, in Jesus Christ, we behold His glory, grace upon grace. He loves us and gives His gifts to us, not because we've deserved them or earned them or can return the favor but because of his love and His gifts and His very essential character of love. He bestows His grace upon His grace, for the sake of His grace—grace for grace, gift for gift, love for love so that our cups overflow. His light shines from the cross at the back of the empty tomb, and men are born anew. God is with us, is for us, has given Himself to us. Death has no claim. We belong, by grace, to God forever. He is begotten of the Father from eternity, but at the time of Caesar Augustus He began as a man, as one of us, our great Emmanuel in the flesh.

Nothing can ruin or stop that. It does not run out. The devil already tried. He could not overcome the light. Grace and truth have come through Jesus Christ, and you are here because Jesus Himself has declared it to you. Here is joy that no one, no thing, can snatch away, which will not fade after time, which cannot be contained in a mere twelve days. Here is joy in the midst of sadness, life in the midst of death, hope in the midst of despair. Here, in Jesus Christ, is God in the midst of men: the Word became flesh.

Our flesh, after His flesh, will receive His reward in due time. In the meantime, we wait and we are at peace. So I am sorry if your Christmas didn't shape up the way you planned or expected or dreamed. I am sorry if it seems as though it whizzed past and you're still sad or lonely. But that doesn't change the facts. The Word became flesh. We have a Savior. Find solace and comfort here. For the Word made flesh is the only stable thing; the only thing that does not age, wither, and die; the only thing that does not disappoint in all of creation. And nothing can ruin that. Therefore nothing can ruin Christmas. The Word became flesh. We have a Savior. Thanks be to God!

In ✠ Jesus' name. Amen.

The Seventh Day of Christmas
The Name of Jesus

December 31

Numbers 6:22-27
Galatians 3:23-29
St. Luke 2:21

In the name of the Father and of the ✠ Son and of the Holy Spirit. Amen.

The faith and worship of the patriarchs revolved around three great observances: circumcision, sacrifice, and Sabbath.

Christ our Lord, named Jesus for He saves His people, observed all three. He was circumcised. He offered sacrifices. He rested and went to the synagogue, or to the temple, on the Sabbath. And in observing them, He also fulfilled them. Even as He reordered and restored His fallen creation, so also He recreated these three observances and gave us something greater. In fulfillment of the three main Old Testament observances, He has given us the three main sacraments of the Church of Jesus Christ: Holy Baptism, Holy Absolution, and the Holy Supper of His body and blood.

Holy Absolution is most parallel to the guilt and peace offerings as well as to the Day of Atonement. The sacrifices cleansed the people and restored fellowship with God. The Holy Absolution purifies the soul of the penitent and strengthens his faith. It forgives the sins that are confessed, and the penitent is freed of his guilt and his shame, welcome to stand in the presence of the Holy God who has loved him and been merciful to him.

The Eucharist stands as the fulfillment of the Sabbath. It is not only the weekly observance of the Church—the place where Christians heed the call of Christ, "O come to Me, ye who are weary and I will give you rest"—but it also echoes the command of the Sabbath, "Remember the Sabbath Day for it is holy," with these words: "Do this, in remembrance of Me." In the Eucharist, we are called to eat and drink in remembrance of the Christ. In the Eucharist, we proclaim His death until He comes again. We are remembering the sixth day, the day when He completed and finished the new creation for us and won for us an everlasting rest.

Holy Baptism is the new creation of circumcision. The Christ had no need in Himself to be cut off from sin or from sinful men. He had no need to be marked as God's own child. But even as the baptism of Jesus does not forgive His sins but infects Him with our sins, that we might be cleansed, so it is that circumcision had the opposite effect on Him as it did on His people. It was the Christ who was cut off. He was sent into the wilderness, consigned to Satan. He was circumcised not simply as an act of humility but also to give power to the promise of all the circumcisions before His. He had been God's own child who had descended to earth and taken up our flesh. Then, on the eighth day, He was marked in that flesh, with His own blood, to be forsaken on the cross. He had been clean of sins, but then the blood that purifies us befouled and defiled Him. His circumcision joins Him to sinful men. He is not marked as God's own child. He is marked instead as the friend and brother of sinners, as one of us, as the guilt offering Himself, the embodiment of sin. And He became a curse that we might be blessed.

Consider how the Lord Himself fulfills this promise from Deuteronomy 30:6: "And the LORD thy God will circumcise thine heart, and the heart of thy seed, to love the LORD thy God with all thine heart, and with all thy soul, that thou mayest live" (KJV).

The Lord circumcises the heart of Israel's seed—that is, of Eve's seed—in order that Israel would love the Lord with all their hearts. The Christ is circumcised in order that His fulfilling of the Law, His perfect love of God and neighbor, would be counted as theirs. He is circumcised that they would fulfill the Law.

Consider also this passage from St. Paul in Colossians 2:11: "In whom also ye are circumcised with the circumcision made without hands, in putting off the body of the sins of the flesh by the circumcision of Christ" (KJV).

You are the circumcised, the chosen people of God, because you have the circumcision made without hands. You have the circumcision made without a knife but instead with water, the stuff of life. You have Baptism. The circumcision of Christ removes the sins of the flesh from the body. How are your sins removed? By Christ's circumcision and by placing Himself under the Law on your behalf, as your substitute and ransom.

This is also what the Litany teaches and confesses. The Litany does not mention the circumcision of our Lord, but it shows that every action of His life on earth was for us men and for our salvation. "By the mystery of Your holy incarnation; by Your holy nativity; by Your baptism, fasting, and temptation; by Your agony and bloody sweat; by Your cross and passion; by Your precious death and burial; by Your glorious resurrection and ascension; and by the coming of the Holy Spirit, the Comforter: Help us, good Lord."

This is also the understanding of the collect of the day: "O Lord God, who for our sakes hast made Thy blessed Son, our Savior, subject to the Law and caused Him to endure the circumcision of the flesh …"

The Father subjected the Christ to the Law and to circumcision for our sakes in order to make us His own, to give us His kingdom, which He bestows by Baptism, Absolution, and the Holy Communion.

Of course His name is Jesus. He saves His people.

In ✠ Jesus' name. Amen.

THE EIGHTH DAY OF CHRISTMAS
THE CIRCUMCISION OF OUR LORD

January 1

Numbers 6:22-27
Galatians 3:23-29
St. Luke 2:21

In the name of the Father and of the ✠ Son and of the Holy Spirit. Amen.

To be born under the Law must mean, in the first place, to be born under the curse. Though our Lord is without the guilt and the concupiscence of original sin, He is nonetheless under its curse. He eats bread by the sweat of His face, and He is returned to the earth upon death. So also, I suspect, to be born under the Law means that St. Mary endured the pain and danger of childbirth because pain in childbirth is key to the curse. It is the essence of the cost of man's rebellion, as that which was meant to be our greatest blessing becomes dangerous and sometimes deadly. And so it is that the Lord's birth redeems childbirth and foreshows the gift of Baptism.

But being born under the Law also means submitting to the Law's many demands. The first of the Law's demands, chronologically for men, is circumcision. Circumcision subjected the circumcised to the conditions of the Law. It brought them into the covenant made with Abraham, which contains both duties and privileges. The Law established a kind of constitutional monarchy. Its threat of punishment was also a promise of justice. But more than that, through this covenant the Lord promised to be the God of the circumcised. That meant that He would hear and answer the prayers of the circumcised and would accept their sacrifices and, most significantly, that He would forgive their sins.

Circumcision stands most parallel to Baptism. The baptism of Jesus did not make Him clean. It made Him dirty. He bathed in our filth.

When He stepped out of the Jordan, the scum clung to Him: He was infected. What is for us the forgiveness of sins is for Him the imputation of sins. So also the circumcision: what joined the people to God cut Jesus off from God. Being cut off allowed all the others to be attached to His Father.

This is the theological principle: He is the Creator. His baptism makes Baptism. His circumcision makes circumcision. We are fairly comfortable with the fact that the Lord instituted these things, but the fact that they have the opposite effect on Him as they do on us is tougher to swallow. It shouldn't be. His death is our life, and our life kills Him. The one exception to this might be His resurrection, for His resurrection is for Him the coming together again of His body and soul. That resurrection inaugurates our own coming resurrections. Since He denied Himself as a man, He rises as man and He is rewarded and elevated to the right hand of His Father as a man. His resurrection and our resurrection are the same. But that, of course, is after He lays down His life, pays the ransom, and pronounces that it is finished. Now we are joined to Him, and what is His is ours and what is ours is His.

In any case, circumcision is a rather nasty piece of ceremony. Consider the near-death of Moses and his salvation at his wife Zipporah's flinty knife.

> At a lodging place on the way the LORD met him and sought to put him to death. Then Zipporah took a flint and cut off her son's foreskin and touched Moses' feet with it and said, "Surely you are a bridegroom of blood to me!" So he let him alone. It was then that she said, "A bridegroom of blood," because of the circumcision. (Exod. 4:24-26)

Moses wimped out. He didn't circumcise his son. This happened, by the way, on their way to Egypt. The Lord had just told Moses that he would be the deliverer. Then this. No transition. Just stated as a matter of fact: "At a lodging place on the way the Lord sought to kill Moses."

Zipporah knows the score: Moses was too wimpy to circumcise his son, so she had to do it. That failure didn't put the boy's life or salvation in danger so much as it put Moses' life in danger.

I use this with parents who delay the baptism of their children. They say to me, "Surely God isn't going to damn my baby because I didn't baptize him." I say, "No, He isn't, but He might damn you." You have a duty to perform. Baptize your children. This also shows us once again how mothers have to step in, Jael- and Deborah-style, and do the father's duty when the father fails. What a terrible thing for Zipporah to have to do! But thanks be to God that she did it. How many of us learned to pray at our mother's skirt? I daresay it is not the exception, though it really should be.

Joseph is stronger than Moses on this. Mary doesn't have to do it. Still, it must have been a terrible thing to circumcise the Messiah. I have full sympathy for St. John the Baptist. Do you really want to anoint the Lord incarnate for death when you aren't even worthy to untie His shoes? If it is tough to circumcise a normal baby, what is it like to place God Himself under the Law and slice Him open? Joseph is a man of great faith. He takes the shame of Mary. He accepts the word of Gabriel in a dream. He is not ashamed to run away from Herod. But maybe this is his greatest courage: he takes the knife and does his duty. Jesus, our Savior, is cut. God be praised!

Joseph seals the infant Lord's fate as surely as John's baptism did. He is cut off from the Lord. He is placed under the Law's condemnation. He sheds His first blood and is anointed to be the Savior of sinful men. His blood is our life. His condemnation is our salvation. His circumcision attaches us to His Father and not only brings in the girls, too, but also completes circumcision. There is no more. It is finished. Now there is Baptism, and Baptism is a far greater thing than circumcision even as the Lord's Supper is a far greater thing than the Passover. When we pine for the Levitical law and the glories of ancient Israel, we are like the Israelites eating manna and quail in the desert but pining for cucumbers in Egypt. The Lord has given us the greater things. Prophets and kings longed for them.

Baptism is greater than circumcision. It is not just for boys. It is not bloody and does not hurt, but don't fail to notice this is: it is deadly. It drowns the old man even as it raises up the new man, and it attaches us to God. See how it fulfills circumcision? It places God's name upon us. Baptism is Baptism because Jesus was baptized, because He was anointed for the sacrifice. As His circumcision ended and fulfilled circumcision and counted for us, so also His baptism began Baptism and counts for us. And since He was born under the Law, we are born above it.

In ✠ Jesus' name. Amen.

The Ninth Day of Christmas

January 2

Isaiah 11:1-5
Galatians 4:1-7
St. Luke 2:22-32

In the name of the Father and of the ✠ Son and of the Holy Spirit. Amen.

The prophecies accompanying Christ's entrance into our world occur not at His circumcision, as with John the Baptist, but at the rites of purification a month later. The Law demanded that the mother and child be purified in the temple with sacrifices. So in came Mary and Jesus.

According to an ancient custom, babies were brought to an old doctor or rabbi in the temple for a blessing. Perhaps it was in that setting that Simeon, being directed by the Holy Spirit, took the Lord Jesus and sang his *nunc dimittis*.

In any case, the Holy Spirit was upon Simeon. In Jewish tradition, this would have meant that he had the gift or spirit of prophecy. According to the rabbis, the Spirit departed from Israel after the prophet Malachi. His return was indicative of the Messianic age.

In the case of Simeon, three specific acts of the Spirit occurred. First, he received direct assurance from the Spirit that he would see the Lord's Messiah before he died. Second, under the influence of the Spirit, he was led to the temple where he recognized Jesus as Messiah. And third, he uttered a prayer and prediction which, in Luke's context, was clearly to be regarded as prophetic.

Simeon had two responses to the Messiah in His arms. The first was a prayer to God. He asked for a peaceful release from this world, and he praised God for the salvation which enlightens Gentiles and glorifies Israel. That part of the song, which we call the Nunc Dimittis, is what we sing each week after the Holy Communion. The second was a prophecy. It was spoken to Mary: "Behold, this child is appointed for the fall and rising of many in Israel, and for a sign that is opposed (and a sword will pierce through your own soul also), so that thoughts from many hearts may be revealed" (Luke 2:34-35).

The mood and theme of the two parts stand in stark contrast to one another. The first part is joyful. It expresses the Messianic hope of the prophets in the person of Jesus the Christ. In the Messiah, even Gentiles will receive the truth of God. They will be enlightened. This will be the glory of Israel, for it will not only reconcile man to God but also man to man. It will bring all of humanity under the fatherhood of Abraham. It will put an end to all war and division. But in the second part, as if to counterbalance the impression of the prayer, praise gives way to warning. What is good for us is terrible for Him. The Messiah, this Jesus, while uniting Jews and Gentiles, will also cause division. He will be rejected by many. This will be accomplished by His suffering and self-sacrifice, which will also bring suffering and sorrow on His mother and His followers.

Being the mother of the Messiah, of God Himself, is the greatest honor bestowed upon any creature, human or angelic, in all of the universe. St. Mary is the most blessed of women, even the most blessed of creation. But it is also a terrible burden. A sword will pierce her soul, even as, to a lesser degree, we are all pierced by the Law. For the death of Jesus Christ shows us the awful price of our sins. This is what justice demands for what we have done: a man, tortured, naked, dying on a cross, betrayed and abandoned by His friends, and, worst of all, forsaken by God, His Father.

But our hearts are pierced that they might be drained of selfish idolatry. They are pierced that we would repent and throw ourselves upon God's mercy. His suffering is not only the price of our sins, what we owe, but also the payment of the same. He dies in our place. He is our ransom and guilt offering. He meets and answers the accusations against us for us. And this horror is not only horror, it is also His glorification, where the Father's love is known and revealed. There His mercy and love meet their purpose, and the Father's will is fulfilled.

The Church's destiny is glorious, but it is also one of conflict. It is the Church Militant, fighting within and under siege from without. No Christian is above his master. We all go the way that He has gone, the way also of St. Mary. These sorrows reveal our hearts. They reveal who we really are. They uncover us. We are not our own; we are His. We belong to Him. He defines us, even as He saves us.

Thus are we bold and eager like Simeon for the end. So, too, do we rejoice in the sorrow of the Messiah that is endured for our joy. Lord, let us depart in peace.†

In ✠ Jesus' name. Amen.

---

† This sermon is dependent upon E. E. Ellis, "Nunc Dimittis" in *New Bible Dictionary*, ed. D. R. W. Wood, I. H. Marshall, A. R. Millard et al., 3rd ed. (Leicester, England; Downers Grove, IL: InterVarsity Press, 1996), 837.

The Tenth Day of Christmas
St. Enoch

January 3

Genesis 5:18-24
St. Matthew 2:13-23

In the name of the Father and of the ✠ *Son and of the Holy Spirit. Amen.*

Enoch, the son of Jared, was the seventh patriarch from creation. He was the father of Methuselah. He lived 365 years. He walked with God. Finally, God took him to Himself. That is really all Moses tells us. St. Luke records his name as an ancestor of Joseph and, therefore, of our Lord.

Hebrews explains what "God took him to Himself" means: "By faith Enoch was taken up so that he should not see death, and he was not found, because God had taken him. Now before he was taken he was commended as having pleased God" (Heb. 11:5).

St. Jude fills us in on Enoch's preaching: "It was also about these that Enoch, the seventh from Adam, prophesied, saying, "Behold, the Lord comes with ten thousands of his holy ones" (Jude 14).

While 365 years seems long to us, in the context of the patriarchs it was brief. Enoch's father, Jared, lived 962 years. Methuselah, Enoch's son, famously lived 969 years. Thus we might count Enoch as having been taken early. If our life spans are 80 years, Enoch's adjusted to our standards would have been somewhere between 25 and 30. His life was relatively insignificant in both the histories of men and the history recorded by Moses. He lived quietly, peacefully, and did not perform great deeds. All he did was preach about the coming of the Lord and walk with God.

He wasn't even a patriarch in the common sense of the word. Seth was still alive and so was Enoch's father, Jared. So he wasn't the old man, the leader. But Enoch did preach to his children. For this alone he is worthy of our praise.

This is also what we should aspire to: to preach the coming of the Lord to our children and to walk with God. But instead we want to be great men. We want to accomplish things. We want to leave a legacy. Repent.

Enoch walked with God, He didn't run with Him. He walked. Faith is a slow and easy thing. It has its moments of intense joy and peace, to be sure, but mostly it is quiet and uneventful. It looks to all the world like the most insignificant of things, like nothing, just quietly teaching your children. Walking with God is not winning glorious battles. It is folding laundry and sweeping the floor and putting away dishes. It simply keeps on, steady. The point is not the destination but the trip, and the point of the trip is the conversation.

There is no better picture of walking with God than the disciples walking to Emmaus on Easter Sunday. As the risen Christ walked with them, beginning with Moses and all the prophets, perhaps pointing out Enoch, He interpreted to them in all the Scriptures the things concerning Himself. He revealed to them that His death and resurrection to atone for the sins of the world was not just an abstract idea but was for them, and their eyes were opened in the breaking of the bread.

To walk with God is to listen to God in His Word and to pray. It is to confess and be absolved. It is to know Him in the breaking of the bread. To walk with God is to be a Christian, which is to be forgiven, to wait on the Lord, to trust that He is good and that His mercy endures forever. Enoch, then, is a model Christian, not just in that he walked with God but also that God brought Enoch to Himself. God took him. This life is not the end. It is not all there is. Enoch, seventh son from Adam, is an example and foreshowing of the resurrection to come. He shows us what is in store. God, in His mercy, will take us whom He counts as great men and saints for the sake of His grace.

In ✠ Jesus' name. Amen.

The Eleventh Day of Christmas
St. Titus, Pastor and Confessor

January 4

Acts 20:28-35
Titus 1:1-9
St. Luke 10:1-9

In the name of the Father and of the ✠ Son and of the Holy Spirit. Amen.

St. Titus was one of Paul's companions. We first learn of him in Galatians 2. He accompanied Paul and Barnabas to Jerusalem for the council that was to discuss circumcision. Titus was himself a test case since he was a Gentile. The council did not compel him to be circumcised and thus the debate was supposed to end for the apostles, but then, like now, it didn't.

We should note that well because we often find ourselves frustrated by the Church's constant struggles. We have this notion that we ought to be able to settle some things and stop fighting, but we don't. It can wax and wane, it can get better and it can get worse, but the Church Militant will always fight, will always struggle. So long as we remain infected by original sin, "church folk" will act badly and hurt one another.

Christians are right to long for the time when they will be relieved, but we should be on guard because Satan can use that desire to embitter us and cause us to abandon the cross. Repent. The disciple is not above his master. This is never going to be easy until it is perfect. Repent and be wary.

Back to Titus. He probably accompanied Paul on his missionary journeys after the council, but no definite information is recorded until the Corinthian crisis. And guess what that crisis was about? Circumcision! Circumcision and dietary stuff just wouldn't go away even though it had already been thoroughly addressed. But, in the way of fallen men, they complicated things and threw in some moral questions and closed communion. Rather than settle any debate, time seems to just pile new twists and issues on top.

Titus seems to have been acting as Paul's representative at Corinth. He was trusted with the delicate task of smoothing over the tense situation between Paul and the Corinthians. He must have been a man of great tact and force of character. He must also have had serious theological aptitude and a willingness to do hard things. He eventually rejoined Paul in Macedonia with good news: the Corinthians had repented. As a result, Paul wrote Second Corinthians, and Titus was given the happy task of carrying that much happier letter to them.

Titus is described by St. Paul as his "partner and fellow worker" (2 Cor. 8:23), who would not think of taking advantage of those entrusted to his care. His final post, after he accompanied Paul to Crete, was to stay in Crete as bishop. There Titus consolidated the Church and ordained pastors. And it was there that he received a letter from Paul to use in that particular work, consolidating churches and ordaining pastors. That letter, of course, we call Titus.

Besides a list of moral requirements for the pastors and bishop, the most striking requirement Paul gives Titus is that pastors and bishops "must hold firm to the trustworthy word as taught, so that [they] may be able to give instruction in sound doctrine and also to rebuke those who contradict it" (Tit. 1:9). Tradition has it that Titus remained in Crete as bishop until his old age, possibly 94.†

The list of qualifications Paul gives Titus fills the hearts of pastors with fear. A pastor is to be above reproach, the husband of one wife, and his children must be believers. He must not be susceptible to the charge

---

† Most of these facts and the order of them come from D. Guthrie, "Titus," in *New Bible Dictionary*, ed. D. R. W. Wood, I. H. Marshall, A. R. Millard et al., 3rd ed. (Leicester, England; Downers Grove, IL: InterVarsity Press, 1996), 1193-94.

of debauchery or insubordination. He is God's steward and must not be arrogant or quick-tempered or a drunkard, nor is he to be violent or greedy for gain. He must be hospitable, a lover of good, self-controlled, and he must also be upright, holy, and disciplined.

If Thou, O Lord, shouldest mark iniquities, who could stand?

Above all, however, as already noted, a pastor must hold firm to the trustworthy word as taught. It is not the only thing, but it is the main thing. "As taught" is what we mean by creedal and confessional. This is also what is trustworthy. Thus St. Paul to Titus:

> But when the goodness and loving kindness of God our Savior appeared, he saved us, not because of works done by us in righteousness, but according to his own mercy, by the washing of regeneration and renewal of the Holy Spirit, whom he poured out on us richly through Jesus Christ our Savior, so that being justified by his grace we might become heirs according to the hope of eternal life. The saying is trustworthy, and I want you to insist on these things, so that those who have believed in God may be careful to devote themselves to good works. These things are excellent and profitable for people. (Tit. 3:4-8)

This is the message, the trustworthy Word, given to Titus to be preached: God our Savior appeared. He was made visible as He took up the flesh of sacrifice from Mary's womb. This He did to save us, according to His mercy. That mercy drives the washing of regeneration and the renewal of the Holy Spirit, which is Holy Baptism. Through Holy Baptism our Lord Jesus Christ pours the Holy Spirit out upon us. Through Holy Baptism He justifies us by His grace to be His heirs.

Titus and all pastors are to insist on these things. What things? The things that God gives for free, by grace, in Holy Baptism: mercy, justification, and His Holy Spirit. Why? So that those who have received them would devote themselves to good works because good works are excellent and profitable for God's people.

Here is an irritant in the Lutheran's mind which could become a pearl. How is it that good works are profitable? Not that they save. They clearly don't. St. Paul tells Titus, in this same sentence, that we are not saved by works done by us, but by God's mercy. The works, however, are profitable. This is how God has intended for us to live. The Law describes what is good. Breaking the law or neglecting good works never satisfies or profits. It always harms. But love does satisfy and profit. In urging the people to devote themselves to what the Law describes, to good works, the Lord is bestowing more blessings upon them, not simply as a burden they must fulfill but mainly as that which is good for them. This He desires not as their ruler and judge, but as their Father, in the same mercy which saved them.

Not by works of righteousness which we have done, but according to His mercy He saved us. We will never fight our way out of this box, out of the Church's struggles and problems. We can't be winsome or clever enough. Heresies must come. The Missouri Synod must be hated within and without, weak and insignificant in the great scheme of things. We won't ever arrive. The same sin that makes our families dysfunctional and which we can't overcome in our own bodies also inflicts the Church. Controversies never quite go away even after they're solved. Yet good works and sound doctrine are profitable. Through these sorrows and struggles God keeps us close to Himself. This is not our Church; it is His. We are not saved by right doctrine or a peaceful veneer and good church management. We are saved by His mercy. There is no escape, no relief, and no peace—except in Him.

This is a trustworthy saying: We are justified by His grace, heirs according to the hope of eternal life. Let us be humbled enough to believe it and be comforted by it and thus follow St. Titus in his following of Jesus Christ.

In ✠ Jesus' name. Amen.

124

The Twelfth Day of Christmas
St. Simeon, Prophet

January 5

Isaiah 63:7-16
St. Luke 2:25-36

In the name of the Father and of the ✠ Son and of the Holy Spirit. Amen.

Thus sings Isaiah:

> I will recount the steadfast love of the LORD,
>   the praises of the LORD,
> according to all that the LORD has granted us,
>   and the great goodness to the house of Israel
> that he has granted them according to his compassion,
>   according to the abundance of his steadfast love.
> For he said, "Surely they are my people,
>   children who will not deal falsely."
> And he became their Savior. (Isa. 63:7-8)

This is the thought of Simeon. For what does this song mean but that God is faithful to His people even when they are faithless? In Simeon's day, things were dark indeed. Herod the Great sat on the throne. The Sanhedrin, the puppet priestly rulers, were utterly corrupt and evil, in bed with whomever was currently in power. Meanwhile, the Pharisees were oppressing the people with legalism and false law. The Holy Spirit had not sent a prophet in the four hundred years since Malachi. Then He lit upon Simeon in the temple, and the Messianic age dawned upon the earth.

Simeon may have known of the fuss at the temple with Zechariah. He may also have known the prophecy we call the Benedictus which Zechariah spoke at John's circumcision. Whether he did or not, by the

Holy Spirit he knew this: Mary's baby Jesus is the Messiah, the Savior who insists that faithless Jerusalem is faithful and will ever be His people. So also he knew that this baby was set for sorrow and suffering and sacrifice.

What Isaiah says is the essence of the Gospel: God declares that sinners are saints in the Christ. This is why Simeon rejoices despite the terrible sorrow of the Christ and St. Mary, why he is hopeful despite the terrible state of the world and the Church in which he lives. The Lord's love is steadfast. His great goodness and mercy are abundant. The Lord who parted the Red Sea and delivered His people from slavery has not changed. Isaiah tells the rebellious Israelites, who hate God and run after idols, that God says, "Surely they are my people, children who will not deal falsely." And in that saying, that holy promise and setting of His will, He became their Savior. He declared sinners to be holy.

What Isaiah sang, pious Messianic believers do in every age: they recount the steadfast love of the Lord which culminates in the Messiah. That is why we sing Simeon's song to this very day, and that is what all the prophets were interested in, what the Psalms sang, what Simeon hoped and waited for. Let it ever be so among us, for so it is also in heaven where the four living creatures, the twelve patriarchs, and the twelve apostles all sing together along with the rest of the saints and the holy angels:

> Worthy are you to take the scroll
>   and to open its seals,
> for you were slain, and by your blood you ransomed
>   people for God
> from every tribe and language and people and nation,
> and you have made them a kingdom and priests to our God,
>   and they shall reign on the earth. (Rev. 5:9-10)

Thus did Simeon hope and depart in peace.

In ✠ *Jesus' name. Amen.*

EPIPHANY

January 6

Isaiah 60:1-6
Ephesians 3:1-12
St. Matthew 2:1-12

In the name of the Father and of the ✠ Son and of the Holy Spirit. Amen.

St. Mary's baby was revealed as God in the flesh to neither the wise nor to the righteous. The shepherds were ignorant outcasts of Jewish blood, despised and untrustworthy—something like our long-delinquent members, Lutherans only in name. They are a type for Jewish believers. Those who are called *wise men* by the ESV are better named as *magi*. They were magicians, pagan (that is, Gentile) astrologers. They looked to the stars for answers and are something akin to palm readers or strippers. They are a type for Gentile believers.

Yet God in the flesh, hiding in humility and sorrow, attracted them both: shepherds and magi, Jews and Gentiles, delinquent members and Ouija board-using addicts. To one set He was revealed by angels in heaven, to the other by a star in the heavens. The birth of the Messiah is the end of our war with heaven, so heaven announces peace and welcomes us home.

Heaven chose as earth's ambassadors two unlikely groups: long-delinquent members with tainted pasts and outright pagans. Thus would heaven confound both those who imagine themselves to be wise and those who think that they are righteous, which is to say that life-long Lutherans and seminary students ought to be both warned and offended. And we all ought to quake and ask, like the apostles at the Last Supper, "Is it I, Lord?" Because it is.

The Lord has come to bring peace and salvation, not to the wise or the righteous; not to those who can quote chapter and verse, recite the Catechism, or sing all the hymns; not to those who serve on the church council or tithe or help in the crisis pregnancy center, but to fools and to sinners. No one great, no one who is mighty in works or knowledge or lineage should exalt himself. And no one weak, dirty, or disreputable, nor anyone divorced, victimized, despised by men, mad at God, doubtful of God's existence, or disgusted with the church should despair. The Lord came for shepherds and magi.

Repent, O Lutherans. The truth, so graciously revealed to you, does not belong to you. It can be taken away, and it certainly will be from those who neglect it. And rejoice, O sinners, you who have nothing in which to boast, who were negligent and took the Word for granted, who forgot your confirmation vows and skipped church, who kept your money for yourself or gave grudgingly. Rejoice, you who sat in the pew and lusted for the girl two rows away or daydreamed of vengeance against co-workers, even as the Word of God was proclaimed. For the Lord reveals Himself as God and man to be a sacrifice, to bestow peace on rebels, to bestow peace on fools and sinners.

Let us not be like Herod, consulting the Scriptures for facts to be used against God or for some trivia while refusing to submit and believe what it says. Let us be instead like the magi and shepherds who hear the call and come to worship, who bask in the humble presence of God in diapers at His mother's breast. There, in her arms, is the peace that passes understanding; there is God's service and offering to man; there is joy worthy of angels and stars. God has taken up our flesh and is born not in Jerusalem, the city of kings, but in Bethlehem, the house of bread. He has made Himself approachable. He does not despise the worship of stinking shepherds and shameful magi. He does not despise sinners. He has come for sinners.

And while we do not rejoice in sins but rather deeply regret and mourn the harm we've done ourselves and one another, let us rejoice in this: He comes for sinners, which is to say, He comes for us. We are not wise or righteous, healthy or put-together. We are sinners: sick, broken, habitual sinners. We need a Messiah, a Savior.

God has provided one—out of Bethlehem and out of Egypt, out of Nazareth and even out of Jerusalem—for He is the scapegoat driven out of the city with our sins upon His head, and He was crucified for us outside the city gates. He comes out of all those places for us.

So there are then no walls to stop you; no pedigree or accomplishments are needed or checked. All you need is to be weary. Come to Me, He says, all who are weary, and I will give you rest. Now there is something we can handle. The Lord who is rest for the weary beckons you to His table.

In ☩ Jesus' name. Amen.

The First Sunday after Epiphany

Isaiah 42:1-7
1 Corinthians 1:26-31
St. Matthew 3:13-17

In the name of the Father and of the ✠ Son and of the Holy Spirit. Amen.

There is a legend, which may or may not be true, about Alexander the Great as a thirteen-year-old boy, taming a horse that no one else could tame. That might seem unlikely until you realize that five years later Alexander would command the cavalry for his father Philip in his conquest of Greece and, shortly after that, would ascend to his father's throne and pretty much conquer the world. In light of that, the description given by Plutarch about the horse is rather believable. Plutarch says that Alexander spoke softly to the horse, turned it so that it faced the sun and no longer saw its shadow, and then took off a fluttering garment he was wearing that might have disturbed the horse. It just might be that Alexander was the first horse whisperer. Whether he was or not, whether the legend is completely false or mostly true, it doesn't matter. It serves its purpose. It shows the character of Alexander: he was a tamer of the world.

The account of the boy Jesus in the temple fulfills a similar purpose. Unlike Plutarch's account of Alexander, there is no doubt for us that St. Luke has got it exactly right, most likely from St. Mary herself. This is what actually happened. It was the custom of our Lord's mother and her husband, after they had returned from Egypt, to go every year to Jerusalem for the Passover. In the year in which our Lord was twelve years old, they had gone as usual. They had assumed that when it was time to go home, the Lord would be in their company. He knew the drill. He knew when they were leaving, and He had never missed before.

He was an obedient boy, ever mindful of His God-given duty in the fourth commandment. He did what He was told. He even anticipated the needs of His parents and others. He never had to be told to share, for example. What is unnatural for sinful men is natural for the Lord made flesh. He was always where He was supposed to be.

That was all still true as He tarried in the temple while they moved on. He didn't fail in this. What was wrong was Mary and Joseph's assumption about where He should be. They thought He should be with them. In fact, they should have been with Him.

This is an important event for the emphasis of the Epiphany season. It is the season of the Lord showing Himself to us, revealing His true, divine character through His humanity. He is present in creation to restore and redeem creation. Even as the Alexander account shows the character of Alexander, this shows the character of the Messiah. He is a Nazarene and the Son of Mary. The prophecies in Isaiah are fulfilled. But He belongs in the city of peace, in His Father's house, the house of prayer for all people.

He is there sitting among the teachers, and they are amazed at how He listens and the questions He asks. When St. Luke records that He was sitting among them, it would be like us saying that He was standing at the podium with the professor or had been invited up on stage with the expert panel. The teachers taught in the temple, sitting, and the students stood. The role that our Lord is playing is subservient, however. Discourse took place through questions and answers. The teachers needed astute students, as sort of apprentice teachers, who would ask the right and truly inquisitive, interesting questions. So He is not just the best student; He is more. And He is recognized as such by the teachers even though He is just barely on the edge of manhood.

He is still a perfectly obedient boy. He is not manifesting His divine nature, but rather His human nature as humanity was meant to be. He is still growing in wisdom and stature. At the tender age of twelve, on the cusp of puberty and adolescence, He is aware of His divine mission, though that too, like wisdom and stature, is growing.

So He asks the right questions of the rabbis which are questions, no doubt, about God's mercy in the Messiah.

And when it gets put to him by His mother, He asks her, "Did you not know that it is necessary for me to be among my Father's things?" I don't think this was a rhetorical question. I think that He really was ignorant of whether she gets it. What He wants to know is if she realizes that He is one of His Father's things and that it is necessary for Him to fulfill the prophecies and promises of His Father. Or was she so caught up in herself that she had forgotten?

All of our translations are weak on this. The formula that Jesus uses is "it is necessary." That formulation should be translated literally because it is an indication of prophecy. It is not an incidental phrase. It shouldn't be paraphrased with the word "must." That is not enough.

Next, He says nothing about either His Father's house or His Father's business. I think this should be rendered very literally as well. What He says is His Father's "things." The translators have taken the context to define what those things are: either an abstraction, His Father's business; or the temple itself, His Father's house. But both miss the point: Jesus identifies Himself with the things of the temple. He identifies Himself not just with the space or the action but with the actual stuff, with the altar, the candle stands, the priests, the sacrifices, the mercy seat, and so forth.

The dead Passover lambs didn't go home with their mothers when the festival was over. Jesus is one of them. Therefore He belongs, rightly, among them. He is one of them and He is all of them. He is the means by which the people will be cleansed. He restores fellowship between God and men and provides safe, gracious access for men to God. He is the temple that will be torn down and rebuilt in three days. He is what will make those who believe in Him temples of the Holy Spirit. And so on.

And then off He goes, back again with Mary, obediently. His hour has not yet come, yet His face is now set toward Jerusalem more than it was before, not according to His omniscience or His divine nature but according to His human nature and self-imposed limits. As a man—a young man, but still a man—He understands what He will do and what will happen to Him. He is one of His Father's things, one of the things the Father uses by destruction and blood to make men holy.

Our problem is that our fallen flesh doesn't want a Messiah who comes to make us holy. We want a Messiah who comes and gives us secret knowledge or power. We want a Messiah who will make us happy, pay our bills, or entertain and amuse us. We think we know better than God what He ought to be and where He ought to be. No matter how we dress it up in our phony Christmas letters, we are frustrated and disappointed by the impurity of our country, our churches, and our families—or else we are delusional. Repent. This world is not our home.

The Lord knows what is best. He doesn't come to make you happy, to make you famous, or to make life easy. He comes to make you His. He comes to restore fellowship with heaven. That is peace on earth, good will toward men. Through the Messiah we are no longer at war with God. We have an advocate and defender. We have a Savior. The boy Jesus in the temple shows us the sad path that He must walk in order to make us His and His simple, unwavering determination to do so. It is necessary. This is the cost and process of love. This is how God loves the world: He sends His Son as a sacrifice.

So maybe you don't walk away today any smarter than you were when you came. You are not now a better parent or employee or even more knowledgeable about the Bible. You don't now know how to organize your basement or pay off your debts. You still live in the same mess, the mess you and others have made. You still have to do the hard work of marriage and parenting and studying. There is not yet an out from office politics, dealing with the in-laws, or cleaning the refrigerator. The only guaranteed difference between how you were when you arrived and how you will be when you depart is that now you are again newly forgiven and will depart in peace.

You belong to Christ. He loves you and is working in and on you. His will will be done. He will get His way. He will bring you home. He will accomplish that for which He was sent. He will die. He will rise. He will ascend. He will open heaven for you.

Alexander didn't tame the world; he put a tiger on a short chain. When he died, the tiger went crazy and the world erupted in violence. But the Lord Jesus Christ submitted to the tiger. He let it destroy Him, and in doing so the tiger lost his teeth and claws and now lies down with the lamb.

Jesus has conquered death. He has conquered hell. He has conquered sin for us. He is one of His Father's things so that you might be one His Father's children.

In ☩ Jesus' name. Amen.

The Second Sunday after Epiphany

Exodus 33:12-23
Romans 12:6-16
St. John 2:1-11

In the name of the Father and of the ✠ Son and of the Holy Spirit. Amen.

On the third day, our Lord went to a wedding in Cana of Galilee where, as His first sign, He gave good wine to drunks.

This is the third day since He called Nathaniel. It is probably the forty-third day since His baptism. He was baptized and then taken immediately to the desert for fasting and temptation. When that was complete, He was ministered to by angels and began His public ministry. He began by calling disciples. Then He went to a wedding and showed His glory so that His disciples believed in Him.

The third day is significant. St. John could have written the next day, or Wednesday, or the day after that, but he wrote "the third day." He wants us to see the connection between our Lord's first sign and the resurrection. He wants us to notice that the first sign takes place in a wedding outside of Judah. He has come to end the divorce: the divorce between men and women, Jews and Gentiles, neighbors and brothers, and also between body and soul. We shall be reunited with God as we were meant to be, at harmony and peace with ourselves, with each other, and with Him. Babel's curse and Adam's curse will both be removed. He provides the wine because He is the true bridegroom.

There is so much here that the most significant thing is usually missed. This is our Lord's first sign. That isn't merely an indication of chronology. It also means that this is His primary, His chief, sign. That means this sign, water into wine, defines all other signs and all of His ministry. He is no John the Baptist, a Nazarite ascetic, fasting in the desert. He did that and overcame. Now He is here and it is time to feast. He comes to weddings. He gives wine, really good wine, to drunks.

The steward takes on a satanic role. He complains that the bridegroom has been stupid and wasteful. Our text translates this as *drunk freely*. The King James has *well drunk*. They are both wrong, or at least they are both misleading. The word here means *intoxicated*. "Everyone serves the good wine first, and when the people are intoxicated, then the poor wine." The steward's complaint is simple: there is no good reason to waste good wine on people who are drunk. The bridegroom is an idiot, criminally negligent and wasteful. These people don't need any more wine. They'll only abuse it. And even if they didn't, their tongues are too numb to appreciate it.

Pay attention! Our Lord is revealing Himself. He is showing His glory. Our text translates, "He manifested His glory." That is right. But in Greek it reads, "He epiphanied His glory." This is where we get the name of the season: Jesus turning water into wine and giving it to drunks at a wedding.

How does this show the Lord's glory? Not by His power in the conventional sense. This sign is not a demonstration that our Lord has control over nature or is powerful. His true glory is not in His ability to turn water into wine. He does that all the time. After all, every bit of wine on earth was once water in a grape. All He has done here, in a sense, is speed things up.

But if His glory is not in His power, then what is it? It is that He gives wine to drunks. He gives good, wonderful gifts to those who in no way deserve them or have the ability to appreciate them, who will almost certainly abuse them. This is His first sign, the primary sign, revealing His character and ministry. It defines all others.

None of this is accidental. It is the third day. They aren't in Judah. They're at a wedding. The people don't understand what they've been given. The jars are also important. The Levitical law only prescribed washing in the case of a nighttime discharge. That didn't require six stone jars of twenty to thirty gallons each. These jars were not to fulfill the Levitical law. These jars were for the guests to ceremonially wash their hands before eating.

There was a problem with that ceremony: some had confused it for what it symbolized. Some of them, like the Pharisees, cared more about an outward keeping of the ceremony than an inward keeping of the Law. There were even jokes about the best of the rabbis knowing of ways to wash creeping things so as to make them clean. The joke was that the Law clearly states that creeping things are unclean, but the rabbis were so clever they could change God's Law with elaborate religious ceremonies. This very thing, hand washing, comes up in regard to our Lord's disciples. The rabbis ask Him, "Why do your disciples break the tradition of the elders? For they do not wash their hands when they eat." His response: "And why do you break the commandment of God for the sake of your tradition?"

Our Lord's first sign, His primary sign and the beginning of His public ministry, does away with rabbinic traditions and abuse. He replaces a phony law with abundant wine. The phony law was meant to make people clean, to keep them from breaking the law and sinning, but it actually misled them into self-righteousness. One response to that is the response of John the Baptist: a call to repentance. That is always in order. But there is another response, a divine response: forgiveness. Jesus eats with sinners. He gives wine to drunks, indiscriminately. He is not John setting the axe to the root. He is the Lamb of God that takes away the sins of the world. The repentance to which John leads us isn't a work we perform to make ourselves worthy. It is the Word of God emptying us, preparing us to be filled.

Repentance and forgiveness, confession and absolution, Law and Gospel: these are two sides or two perspectives of the same divine Word and will. We are drunks, gluttons, and perverts. We should be struck down for our crimes, but the Lord pours out mercy and love upon us.

He welcomes us, declares us His own children and bride. He declares us holy and immaculate and good. All of His signs, all of His ministry, fit this pattern and continue this mission. That is His glory: He gives good wine to drunks.

Two more things. First is St. Mary's faith. She comes to our Lord with a complaint: "They have no wine." She does not say what she wants Him to do, but clearly she wants Him to do something. We aren't told why she cares or what she expects. In any case, she is rebuked for this. His hour has not yet come. But she has faith. She does not let go. The rebuke does not crush her. She prays and is told "no." But she still trusts. She expects something good from Him, something good and undeserved from God, for she knows that He is good and she knows that He will provide. "Whatever He tells you to do, do it" is a marvelous confession. That is what faith looks like, faith that leads to drunks getting good wine.

Second is this: His disciples believed in Him. That is the purpose of His revelation, of this epiphany. He reveals Himself to them, to the disciples, to us, to those who believe in Him. His purpose is to gather the elect, His flock. He is not desperate, not trying to make it work to gain profit or prestige. He is not trying to convince them or argue them into the kingdom.

The church is failing and is in decline. On this side of glory, it always is. Only the devil prospers fully. Here Christians always suffer, for they go the way of their Master to the cross. Yet in the midst of that suffering, the Lord brings joy, feasting, and the Holy Spirit. He reveals Himself to His disciples, and they believe in Him. He makes their hearts glad.

On the third day, our Lord went to a wedding in Cana of Galilee where, as His first sign, He gave good wine to drunks. Oh, taste and see that the Lord is good!

In ✠ Jesus' name. Amen.

The Third Sunday after Epiphany

2 Kings 5:1-15
Romans 12:16-21
St. Matthew 8:1-13

In the name of the Father and of the ✠ *Son and of the Holy Spirit. Amen.*

From the Mount of Beatitudes came again our Lord to Capernaum. There He encountered the good centurion, who had learned to love Israel and her God and had built them a synagogue. The good centurion represents the end of Judaism. It is not merely that they are occupied by a foreign army but also that the center of God's people is shifting from Jerusalem—from that temple built with hands, from Palestine—to Him who lays down His life and takes it up again, who is a house of prayer for all people in the fullest sense of the term. The old boundaries of the Law—that is, the boundaries of the old temple, the boundaries between Jews and Gentiles, men and women, priests and laity—are being dissolved in the person of Jesus Christ.

Therefore the good centurion goes not to feast with Alexander, Scipio, and Caesar, but with the heroes of the Christian faith. He goes to feast with Abraham, Isaac, and Jacob. They are now his kin. He calls Abraham *father* for he is a child raised up from a stone.

In contrast, those who had only an outward connection with Abraham would discover it was not enough. The distinctive thing about Abraham was not his curly hair or great learning, nor was it the outward circumcision. The distinctive thing about Abraham was his faith. He hoped and waited for the grace of God in the Messiah, for the forgiveness of sins and reconciliation to the Father. To be a son of Abraham is to be circumcised in the heart and washed in the blood of the Lamb.

Those who thought they were sons of the kingdom by right were wrong. No one, including the good centurion, is fit or worthy of this.

The kingdom is bestowed by grace upon the undeserving, or not at all. Those who think they come by right—whether that is because they were baptized in the Missouri Synod, because they served on the church council, or because their mother was Jewish—will all be cast into the outer darkness where there will be weeping and gnashing of teeth.

Weeping comes from sorrow. Gnashing of teeth is not due to anguish or physical torture, but rather anger or rage. They wanted to go their own way on this earth, to be their own lords. They insisted they be judged and handled according to their own history and righteousness, so they will be. They will be given over precisely to what they desired and shall spend eternity in their own sin, in darkness. They will spend eternity in sorrow and in frustrated, debilitating anger, in weeping and gnashing of teeth.

This shows us how terrible anger is. In hell men are given over to their anger. There is nothing, no one, to mediate them from themselves. There is no Law, only wrath, and they are alone.

Anger is probably the most acceptable sin in our culture. We give in to it all too easily. It has a vain air of strength. I saw a bumper sticker once, washed in red, white, and blue, that said something like "No comfort or aid to the enemy—ever!" with a big exclamation point. That sentiment is in direct contradiction to our Lord's command that we love our enemies. But it makes us feel good for a brief moment to pound our chests and strut around and talk about vengeance, only we probably don't use that word. But vengeance, even if we call it justice, is what we want. Vengeance is mine, saith the Lord. That means it is not yours. And if you take by force what is the Lord's, you will be damned.

We mostly recognize the man who is overcome by drunkenness or lust as a slave. But we mistakenly think that the wrathful or angry man is strong. He is not. He is just as much a slave as the others, maybe worse, because his sin is more directly tied to pride. All sinful anger is tinged with more than a little self-righteousness, as though the injustices and slights you've suffered were cosmically significant and the whole universe ought to stop on your behalf. How dare someone cut in front of you in traffic! Don't they know how important you are? How dare someone be rude to you, of all people, at the grocery store!

The Holy Spirit does not move us to anger, but to pity. The Lord describes hell as being full of people whose pride led them to think that God owed them something because they belonged to the right club or knew the secret word. He describes hell as a place where people will gnash their teeth and make themselves angry without relief.

Here is the point: Giving in to anger and being angry is to bring upon yourself a little hell on earth now. Stop it. Repent. Let it go. Turn. To give in to anger is to gnash your teeth against God, to insist on your own way, to demand your own vengeance. You only hurt yourself and those you love. Your anger is weak and unhealthy. Most importantly, it is dangerous to the health of your soul. Repent.

Consider the good centurion. He is strong, but his strength is in virtue. He is strong in faith, hope, and love along with patience, humility, and wisdom. What happens to the good centurion's servant physically is an illustration of what had happened already to the good centurion spiritually. The Lord worked physical healing and life in the servant, from afar, by His Word. He had done the same spiritually for the good centurion. The centurion was unfit in a Levitical sense, and unworthy in a moral sense, but the Lord healed his soul with His Word. He gave him not a new place, not a new thing, but the place that is bestowed upon faith through grace: a place with Abraham, Isaac, and Jacob, a place in the kingdom. That is really something and it is quite explicit. The centurion is healed, is reconciled, and is loved by God.

No wonder, then, that his prayer has been taken up by the Church as the traditional prayer before receiving the body of Christ. We are not worthy or fit that Christ enter into us. We are morally impure because we have sinned. We are ceremonially unclean because we are distracted, lacking in proper fasts and discipline, unprepared. But the Lord says, "Take, eat, this is My body," so we do, at His command, as men under authority. And our souls are healed, not from afar but near, by His Word joined to bread to be His body for us. Thus are we joined to the death and resurrection of Jesus Christ. He enters into us and gives a place with Abraham, by faith, and makes us partakers, temples even, of the kingdom and the Spirit and the Christ.

This is the real miracle in Capernaum. Yes, the centurion and his servant are healed. But that is not the chief thing or the chief miracle. It is not even the centurion's faith. The chief miracle is Christ. Christ Himself—His grace, His undeserved love, His mercy—is the miracle. He is the kingdom. He is the hope of Israel. He is the Savior of Gentiles. He is giver of faith and the creator of Christians, making us brothers, daughters, and brides all in one glorious word: It is finished.

In ✠ Jesus' name. Amen.

The Fourth Sunday after Epiphany

Jonah 1:1-17
Romans 13:8-10
St. Matthew 8:23-27

In the name of the Father and of the ✠ Son and of the Holy Spirit. Amen.

J esus can sleep through anything. He has no fears, no guilt, no worries. Sometimes it seems as though He sleeps through our prayers. In any case, He rarely behaves the way we think He should. Why was He sleeping while the storm raged? Why was He not with His disciples, teaching or praying or comforting them? Why wasn't He helping? And why, when they came to Him looking for salvation, did He rebuke them? He had praised Gentiles for the same request.

Perhaps there is no more important theological lesson to learn than this: God is not like us. He does not submit to our ideas. His ways are not our ways. His thoughts are not our thoughts. We live by faith, not by knowledge or understanding.

Unlike every other man, Jesus never considers appearances. He really doesn't care what people think. He is His own man in a way that no one else is, that no one else can be. He is not concerned with doing the proper thing. He simply is. And whatever He does, whether we understand it or not, is the right thing.

That idea requires faith because He doesn't seem to be doing the right thing very often. He seems to be sleeping, to be ignoring us. Wars and disease, hatred and greed, bigotry and addiction: these things don't seem right and yet they are all around us. We are plagued with crime and poverty. Families are falling apart. Babies are murdered in their mothers' wombs. American soldiers die in foreign lands while wives at home are unfaithful. The government lies. Children cheat. Schools can't be trusted. Friends betray us. Pastors preach false doctrine.

And then, as if we weren't already our own worst enemies, nature herself comes swooping down upon us in hurricanes and tsunamis, in killing frigid temperatures, in ice and snow. And all our efforts against these things—our little programs for grief and debt, our attempts to counsel pregnant teens and marriages in distress, our engineering feats and government money—all of it seems of little effect against the evil that lurks in the hearts of men or the waters that fill Lake Pontchartrain or the killing waves and wind that come crashing into Japan. They are futile, like wrapping gauze over the top of a volcano to stop the lava.

These vain efforts of men would lull us to Jonah's denying sleep. They would placate us with Utopian fantasies. Make no mistake. If *Leave it to Beaver* and *The Cosby Show* now seem cliché and transparent, if Hallmark seems obviously sappy and Martha Stewart seems just plain fake, then turn to any home improvement show or even to a cooking show. Those are pure fantasies disguised as reality. No one lives like that. But they are barometers of our discontent. They show what we want but fail to obtain, what we think the world should be like but isn't. Repent.

Your answer doesn't lie in gadgets or flower bouquets, in a beautiful home or a beautiful meal. Nor does it rest in happy, healthy, well-adjusted children. And there is no such thing as Harlequin's soulmate either. You won't find salvation in human love. Spouses and children disappoint as surely as parents and siblings, as surely as we disappoint ourselves. Repent. Stick to your prayers. Submit in faith to the goodness of God and wait for the Lord. It will be revealed in time. The storms will cease. Jesus is with you, whether the centerpiece looks like Martha's or the faucet drips or not.

And what if the Lord rebukes you for your panic and discontent, for your desire for safety, for your desperate little faith that thinks it is perishing? Thanks be to God! Thanks be to God that you still have a smoldering wick of faith and that it knows where to go, that it still prays, that it seeks salvation in Jesus' name. Thank God you are weak, for then you are strong. He will not let you become dependent on your faith or upon your works or upon your visions of this world. He will purify you with holy chastisement. He will prevent you from riding out the storm in false confidence. Thanks be to God, He is keeping and will keep you dependent on Him.

And what if your conscience is plagued by guilt and regret, by doubt and fear? What if you are weary? Thank God for that as well. For it is faith, a living and vibrant faith, that stirs your heart. Faith causes you to feel sorrow and shame, not doubt or unbelief. The pain is proof that your faith is alive. Pray that you never lose that feeling until God relieves you of it on the last day. Pray that you are never comfortable in your sins, that you never think you've got Him figured out, that you can handle the storms on your own.

Be rebuked again and again. Suffer His insults. Be broken by His Law. For in this way He empties you of yourself in order to fill you with His love. He breaks you to mend you. He kills you to revive you. For His sake we are killed all day long! God be praised for it. We are counted as sheep for the slaughter. God be praised, His thoughts are not our thoughts.

If we stop feeling the Law, we lose the Gospel. First comes the rebuke, then comes the calming of the storm. First comes the cross, then comes the glory.

Are we of little faith, O Lord? Indeed. We are unworthy in every way. But You have made a promise. You are our God. Your name is upon us. Save us, O Lord! Be our God, our Savior. Deliver us from these present evils and from the evil one. Count us in that rag-tag, fearful group on Lake Galilee. Let us also be your failing disciples, that you might show Your grace in us. We have no boast, no claim upon Your mercy, but we have Your Word and promise. That is enough. You will be our Jonah, O sleeper. You will calm the sea with Your sacrifice, for You have gone into the belly of the earth and come forth again on the third day. Rebuke us if You must, send the waves over the sides of the boat, make us desperate and full of fear, and teach us to pray. And then, O Lord, give us peace according to Your Word. Give us the faith we lack. Give us Your Holy Spirit and bring us home. Remember, O Lord, Your Word and promises even while we wait for the resurrection to come and the consummation of all our hope. Save us, O Lord. Save us.

In ✠ Jesus' name. Amen.

THE FIFTH SUNDAY AFTER EPIPHANY

Genesis 18:20-33
Colossians 3:12-17
St. Matthew 13:24-30

In the name of the Father and of the ✠ Son and of the Holy Spirit. Amen.

Almost as bad as the enemy who sowed bad seed among the good are the servants of the sower. They accuse him of having sown the bad seed. That is blasphemous, and their solution is arrogant to the point of being utterly ridiculous. They think he goofed it up and he needs them to go and fix it.

The sower is God. His servants are the preachers. It is the preachers who do not believe God's Word is good enough, that since there are weeds the Word must be flawed and thus requires their adjustment. They are also impatient with God's *kairos*, with His time. They want to fix it themselves, and they think that they have lots of solutions.

As it was then, so it is to this day. Repent.

The parable of the wheat and tares demonstrates the foundational difference between Islam and Christianity. It is not our job to end unbelief. We are not trying to usher in heaven on earth. Mohammed's god rejoices at the death of infidels. He even demands their slaughter. But the God of Abraham takes no pleasure in the death of the wicked, and He prays for those who murder Him. When the Son of Man, who sows good seed upon the earth, is asked by His foolish servants if they should weed the garden, He tells them, "No. Don't pull the weeds. Don't try to get rid of sinners. Don't try to end war or poverty or hunger or divorce. Don't try to save the lost."

These are hard words for preachers.

God has not instituted a purifying cult. He sends Jonah to Nineveh, not for vengeance but to preach repentance, to offer salvation to the Gentiles. Jonah doesn't go to make a sales pitch. He isn't opening franchises. He just preaches, even if he doesn't want to, and God saves the lost.

The Lord does not destroy Egypt either. Rather, He calls His people out of it. Only those who pursue His people through the sea are destroyed.

But what of the Canaanites? They were interlopers. They came into the vacuum left by Jacob's sojourn in Egypt. That land was not theirs. Even there, though, we see mercy. They should have all followed the example of Rahab, who is not only spared but also brought into the family.

No one comes to the kingdom by right. Everyone who calls Jesus *Lord* does so by the Holy Spirit. Abraham believed and it was reckoned unto him as righteousness. God is patient in His mercy. He leaves the tares for mercy's sake.

But beyond the distinction between us and the Muslims, or the social justice crowd, there is a personal dimension here as well. The reign of God's Son, the Messiah, has begun. That is what St. John pronounced. We have lost some of the original nuance of the word *kingdom* in English. The kingdom of heaven is likened here to a man who sows good seed, whose enemy then comes along and sows weeds on top of it. That which St. John announced is better translated *kingship*. It is not the territory. It is the rule. Better yet, it is the ruler. The Lamb of God is the king, the ruler. His reign has begun as evidenced by the signs He performs, by the widespread inclusion of Gentiles, and by His preaching.

It has begun, but it is not yet complete. This—for the wheat, for the sons of the kingdom—is highly frustrating. The day will come when there will be no kings or presidents, or whatever we call them, upon the earth. Jesus will rule alone. His kingdom of power and glory will be evident to all creation. Then every knee will bow and every tongue confess that He is Lord, even the knees and tongues in Sheol and Gehenna.

But now there are other kings. Satan himself, the enemy of all that is good, of all that is God, claims for himself the title *prince of this world*, even though the reign of God in the Christ has begun. There are also Herods and Augustuses, even Davids and Solomons. They will not last. They will hand over their crowns, but not yet. And so we wait.

Our sins have been forgiven through the sacrifice of Jesus Christ, but like earthly kings and tyrants they still abide in us. We are infected with the curse of Adam. We are broken and depraved even as we are declared at the same time to be the Lord's own saints, His holy ones. The good work has been begun in us. It now lives by faith even as the old man in us fights for all he is worth. We desperately want it to be over. We want to be complete. We want to be free of lust, greed, and pride. We want to stop our shameful ways. We want to be pure as we are declared to be.

Here is the thing, then: the tares are not just outside, growing up next to us, but they are also inside of us. Doubt and anger grow up alongside of faith. Greed and lust temper all our charity. And the good that we would do, we do not do, but we do the things that we hate. And in our childish, selfish, fallen flesh we cry out in frustration: "Why God? Why give us the glimpse of the beatific vision but leave us in this flesh?" Or worse, we don't cry to God at all. We simply make our plans, write our books, and vainly try to fix it by ourselves.

Repent.

Thanks be to God for His enduring patience. We deserve nothing but punishment. He is wise. We are fools. We understand little of grace and the Gospel. We are always trying to be active instead of passive. The Lord sows good seed, His holy Word, despite the enemy, knowing full well the cost. He comes to redeem and purify the earth and the inhabitants of the earth, every beast and bird and creeping thing, and every son and daughter of Adam. But He will purify and purge, He will harvest and thresh, in His own time.

He will complete the good work begun in you when the time is best. You are baptized. He has made His claim. The enemy cannot have you, but He is merciful and works all things together for good. He sees the tares in your heart and does not destroy your faith in order to be free of your sin. He is merciful.

Where the fallen flesh is frustrated and angry, the new man is simply thankful. This patience is not weakness; it is mercy. Whatever besetting sins beset us, we have not been given over to them or destroyed by them, as would be just. We have done terrible things. Sometimes there have been consequences: jail, divorce, financial penalties, embarrassment, the loss of a job, and who knows what else. But all in all, we've been mainly spared. We have not paid much for our sins even when we've had to face up to some temporal consequences. Jesus has paid for them for us, not only temporally but also eternally. We have gotten away with incredible amounts of sin, punished only where it was necessary, not in wrath but in mercy, for our good, as a father chastises and disciplines his sons.

But we have more than mercy and fatherly discipline. We also have grace. We are not merely spared punishment, but we are also elevated. We are declared to be God's own family, His children and His bride. This is how He reveals Himself again and again. He is the one who rules us by laying down His life upon the cross. He is the one who loves not only us but all of humanity, the one who says, "Do not weed the garden."

There is a strange bit of good news in our Lord's prophecy: "The poor you will have with you always." There are poor. There is hunger. There is war. Those are the fruits of the tares. But for us they are opportunities for mercy. They are not problems to be fixed. They can't be fixed. It is not your job to end poverty or save the lost or get men to stop divorcing their wives. You can't fix it and aren't expected to. It is not your burden. Your job, your burden if we can call it that, is to receive God's grace and praise His name. It is your job to be forgiven.

"What shall I render unto the LORD for all his benefits toward me? I will take the cup of salvation, and call upon the name of the LORD" (Ps. 116:12-13). That is your job. Nothing more. Relax and rejoice. The Lord will provide. The Lord will save. Even you the Lord will save. He will bring the harvest home. He will end the pretend reign of His and our enemy. He will reveal to all creation that you are His son or daughter. He will remove the plank from your eye and the tares from your soul without harming you.

In ✠ Jesus' name. Amen.

Transfiguration

Exodus 34:29-35
2 Peter 1:16-21
St. Matthew 17:1-9

In the name of the Father and of the ✠ Son and of the Holy Spirit. Amen.

Part of the problem with being such magnificent and well-seasoned liars is that we are constantly losing track of our own fabrications. It is bad enough that we can't tell the simplest story without exaggeration and embellishment, if not flat out falsehood, but what is worse is that half the time we get so caught up in our malarkey that we ourselves believe it. When we are called on it, we act as though our honor had been sullied, not by the lie, but by the accurate accusation.

We are delusional. Sin makes us stupid. We have no right to look down on Lance Armstrong or Richard Nixon or Martha Stewart.

What we care about most is our reputations, which is to say, what people think of us. We care a lot, way more than makes any sense. Almost all of our lies stem from this. We want to be liked, respected, and admired. Why else would we care about honor?

This base desire is hard to admit. Thus we spend a lot of time lying about it, claiming that we don't care what people think. In fact, we not only care, but it is no exaggeration to say that we are actually terrified of what people think. That is why we lie. We lie because we want people to think better of us than they should or than we deserve. We lie to try to impress them or to hide our shame.

We are an incredibly fearful people. We are afraid of our neighbors, afraid of crime, and afraid of genetically-modified wheat. We are afraid of the District President, afraid of our congregations, and afraid of getting caught in our secret sins. We are afraid of practically everything, but we deny it. We deny it all. We pretend to be brave, tough, and calm. We hate to admit fear, no matter how much it wracks us, because it makes us look weak. We are all still little boys in the locker room: afraid of being made fun of, beaten up, or, even worse, afraid of looking stupid, failing, or being rejected. But that which haunts us the most, even though we rarely admit it even to ourselves, is death and judgment.

Repent. It is time to confess and come clean. You have been afraid of almost everything except God.

And if this isn't ringing true, if you really are calm all the time and don't get excited or afraid, if you don't have any secrets or things you lie about, then the Bible isn't written to or about you. The Bible isn't addressed to calm, cool people. It is written to cowards. Every time some poor slob runs into an angel, he has to be told, "Don't be afraid." Fear is the constant reaction of sinful human beings in the presence of holiness.

Thus our Lord to Peter, James, and John at His transfiguration: "Don't be afraid." They are right to be afraid. For a minute there, Peter lost his mind. He thought he was the pope, the first of the apostles and on equal footing, at the least, with Moses and Elijah and maybe even with God Himself. He is a man with a plan. He speaks right up: "Let's stay here."

But when the Father speaks from heaven, Peter recognizes his frailty and sin. He is not much different than Moses blowing it at Meribah or not circumcising his son. He is not really any more pious than Elijah was under the broom tree. Peter is afraid for his life. For if angels are terrifying to sinners, and they are, then the divine presence is deadly. So Peter falls on his face, afraid.

The gentle, patient response of our Lord can't be overstated. The divine presence of God in the man of the Messiah is terrifying, but He is no longer deadly to sinners. In the man Jesus, come to be a sacrifice, the divine presence is sanctifying and life-giving. The mercy that endures forever has flesh. So the rebuke on the mountain is gentle.

We should probably translate what the Father says with a paraphrase like "Be quiet" or even "Shut up" and then "Listen to My beloved Son." It is a serious admonition, but there is no malice in it. It is, in fact, serious encouragement. Thus the next words they hear are pure Gospel: "Don't be afraid. Arise."

Then, at the word and touch of Jesus, they have eyes only for Jesus. Moses and Elijah might still be there. Nothing is said about whether they have departed or become invisible, but now, for a brief moment of sanity, Peter, James, and John are lifted out of themselves. They are no longer afraid for their reputations, needing the approval or praise of Moses or one another. Nor are they even afraid to go to Jerusalem and die. For a moment, they bask in the pure, accepting grace of Jesus Christ and know that He is good and gladly rest in His will.

That same mercy provides even us poor, miserable liars and self-promoters with similar moments of clarity and honesty. Thank God for that! There are times, by grace, when our duties are light, when it is easy to love God and neighbor. But even when we spurn them and go about our lying lives and boastful ways, the Lord is steadfast. His face is set toward Jerusalem even as we are trying to figure out a way to stay on the mountain. He is always proceeding for our good. Heaven is populated with liars like Abraham and Isaac and Peter who have found grace in the Messiah. Thanks be to God for that! There is even room for us.

May God, in His mercy, give us today, through the Sacrament, eyes only for Jesus and faith to see us through to the end.

In ✠ *Jesus' name. Amen.*

MOVEABLE
DAYS

Sunday within the Octave of Christmas

Isaiah 11:1-5
Galatians 4:1-7
St. Luke 2:22-40

In the name of the Father and of the ✠ Son and of the Holy Spirit. Amen.

This child, hunted by Herod, rejected by the innkeeper, is set for the falling and rising again of many in Israel. Everything will be measured by this standard. He is all that matters. Many will reject Him. They will not fall upon Him and be broken, so He will fall upon them and crush them on their pride. Repent.

You, by God's grace, will be broken. You will be and are crushed by the Law, slain, cut to the heart. Your old nature has been drowned with Him and buried in Holy Baptism. You have risen from that watery grave, by the power of the Holy Spirit, to life. If you live, you live in that baptism or not at all.

The old man in you is, again and again, fighting for supremacy. He nurses old grudges. He complains about the slightest inconvenience. Day by day, constantly, again and again, he must be drowned by contrition and repentance. You confess anew, "Forgive us our trespasses." The new man is raised by grace. He is called out, called back, revived in the Holy Absolution. He is fed and nourished in the Holy Communion. He is seen in the Word—revealed as the Lord's own man, the new man in Christ's image—and felt in the heart.

You are broken but mended, fallen but risen, dead but alive. You are a penitent saint, which is the only kind of saint. This is the life of faith. The old thoughts are purged from your black heart, and the thoughts of His pure heart are placed there. Those thoughts, those perfect thoughts of God's own Son, are your thoughts in Him who gave His life for you. You are righteous for He is righteous. You bear His name and you belong to Him.

This is how faith is lived on this side of glory. You follow the model of faith: Lady Israel, Holy Mother Church, St. Mary herself. That is why your heart is sword-pierced and broken. That is why sin hurts. Rebellion never serves. You see in yourself, in your heart, the selfish thoughts of the man who sent Christ to hell. You see that you are the cause of the terrible cost that He bore. You drove Him out of Bethlehem. You bore false witness against Him. You crucified Him. If that is not enough to break your heart, nothing is.

But even if it is broken, it is St. Mary's heart. Look to the Word. See there that the cause of Christ's sorrow was just as much the faithful love of God as it was your sin. He desired to win you back. He counted you worthy. He wanted you. And He holds no grudge. He loves you. This is how He loves the world; the death of Jesus, His unjust condemnation, and His innocent suffering are the cost of His love.

The child we adore, the beloved of the Father, is a sign that is spoken against. The suffering He endured to purify and cleanse you, He asks you to also endure in some measure. So you also become a sign that is spoken against. In the first place, you speak against yourself in your heart. You confess that you are a sinner, that you do not deserve God's pity, that you wish to do better.

And you also face ridicule and shame in the world. Speak up in the work place or the family reunion about the immorality of homosexuality or the lie of evolution, and you will know what it is to be a sign spoken against. Yet this sorrow does not cleanse you. It is not meritorious. You do not do it to work something off. Christ has paid your entire debt. There is no punishment for sins. He has borne it all. Certainly, your sorrows are not in any way the price of years off an imaginary purgatory.

So why the suffering? Your Father places a cross upon you to discipline you. You are His disciples. You are to put your hand to the plow and not look back. You are to pick up your cross, to suffer the loss of friends and family, the shame and scorn of righteousness, like St. Mary before you. He also burdens you with the inability to enjoy your sins and with the constant need to return again and again to the house of the Lord. You must come back for cleansing and restoration. You are utterly dependent upon Him who has broken you. You live by and for His Holy Word and Sacraments and count all else as nothing for the salvation that is in you. His life, death, and rising are the cause of your own life, death, and rising. Nothing else matters and nothing else satisfies.

Holy discipline comes from heaven upon those whom He loves. You will learn through your crosses, through suffering, that He is all that matters. A sword will pierce your heart. He takes away your hiding places, your excuses. He exposes the thoughts of your heart, that you might learn anew that there is no other place to turn, no other consolation, no other hope. You can't hide in your heart or thoughts or deeds. You can't hide in your ancestors or doctrine or friends. So you cry for mercy, for atonement, and you are cleansed in the blood of Christ. You are spared and God is pleased.

Crushing and painful though it is, in this way your evil thoughts are expunged, taken away, forgiven. You confess and are absolved. You kneel before His body and blood and are united in Him who is perfect in His body and blood. You hear His voice in His Word. You know the truth: in Him, you are free. He will never leave you nor forsake you. He loves you.

In ✠ Jesus' name. Amen.

The Second Sunday after Christmas

Genesis 46:1-7
1 Peter 4:12-19
St. Matthew 2:13-23

In the name of the Father and of the ✠ Son and of the Holy Spirit. Amen.

A voice is heard in Bethlehem. It is Rachel weeping for her children. She says, "They are no more." Herod took their lives in his vain attempt to cast a net big enough to catch God. But God escaped in the night. He was exiled to Egypt, the land of slavery and infanticide. Meanwhile, the women of Bethlehem had their boys snatched from their arms and put to cruel death.

Why didn't God warn their husbands as He had Joseph? It is a fair question, and it sits behind Rachel's refusal for comfort. She is mad at God. In reply, God says, "Refrain your voice from weeping and your eyes from tears, for your work shall be rewarded. Do not say, 'They are no more,' for they are with Me."

Why would Rachel refuse that? She refuses it because she wants to indulge her sadness and depression. The sad reality is that we lack the discipline and charity required to get on with life. We enjoy complaining and drawing attention to ourselves. We bask in the illusion that we are worthy of pity. We have all of the emotional maturity of a two-year-old throwing a tantrum. We smash the television because Bambi's mother dies and we refuse to watch anymore. Repent.

God has given you many good things. He sustains you in them still. Will you dare to refuse the comfort He gives? Will you turn your back on your wife, child, and neighbor for vanity and pride just to prove to everyone how unjust your sorrow is? Are these things—these relationships, people, and vocations—which God has provided not enough? Must you insist on your own way and be driven by lust and ego to the pit of death? Do you really think you can see for yourself what is good for food, pleasing to the eye, and capable of making one wise?

Repent. Turn back. Stop this foolish ego trip. Your tantrums and delusional sadness destroy those who love you. Your anger at God, your anger at yourself, is misplaced. God desires to comfort you. He has good news. Will you listen?

He promises Rachel, "Your children shall come back from the land of the enemy. There is hope in your future. Your children shall come back to their own border." It is true also for you. Do not mourn as those who have no hope. What God takes away, He restores. "Your children shall come back from the land of the enemy. There is hope in your future. Your children shall come back to their own border."

There is sadness now and much of it is unjust. The way we love those who have died is by mourning. We might feel some small sadness when we hear of a child dying of hunger in Ethiopia, but we don't mourn for that child because we didn't know him, didn't love him. We mourn for those we love. It is how we keep loving them.

And you are a victim in many ways. All our sins, both the things we do wrong or leave undone and the sin which we have inherited from Adam, have awful consequences. David loses the son by Bathsheba. Stephen is stoned by those he loves. But we do not mourn as those who have no hope. We have hope. Jesus Christ did not stay in Egypt. He came out of the land of slavery. He crossed the Jordan with the sign of the dove and the opening of heaven. He went to the cross. He rose from the dead.

Thus you have hope. Your God is not the god of the dead. Abraham lives. So do Moses, Elijah, and Malachi. So do the boys from Bethlehem, slaughtered while Jesus escaped in the night. They live because Jesus lives. They have come back from the land of the enemy. They have been reunited with their mothers. If their mothers endured fifty years of sadness here on earth without them, which is no small thing, they have now enjoyed two thousand years in perfect union in heaven and are looking forward to an eternity still to come. They will never be separated and never be sad again.

Thus it is written: Our present sufferings do not compare to the glory that will be revealed in us.

I know you are sad. I know you are hurting. But do not think that the forgiveness of sins you have received, that your baptism, that God's promises are insignificant or too small for your problems, sins, and suffering. Do not say, "What good is it if God loves me but my husband or sister or child is gone?" The forgiveness of sins does not yet remove all your aches and pains. It does not yet take away all your sadness, doubts, and fears. Not yet. But you have hope. God is not yet done with you. He will bring it to completion in the day of Jesus Christ.

That is why you are called to live by faith, not by what you see or feel or think, but by every Word that proceeds from the mouth of God. You are righteous in the sight of God for Jesus' sake. And you live in the eager expectation of a watchman waiting for the morning, eager for the rising sun. And if it is the case that your mourning causes you to long for the end, to be detached from this world, God be praised, because the love of money is the root of all evil. Desire to be free of this world and to be with your Lord and your loved ones, to be dissatisfied with earthly things, is a good and holy desire. It is hope.

If you drew a line on the map to show the path of the Israelites called out of Egypt through the desert on their way to the Promised Land and stopped even a day short, you'd never be able to tell where it was leading. They wandered all over the place. Their tracks looked like they were going in every direction except toward the Promised Land. But God brought them there. And the Lord remembers you. There is no good luck and there is no bad luck. He works all things together for good. He is leading you home, no matter how wandering and convoluted the journey.

The boys from Bethlehem died that night so that Jesus would escape and return to die for them. His martyrdom liberated them out of this living death. It relieved them early of their burdens. It was not as it may have appeared. It was not that their lives were exchanged for His; it was His life given in exchange for theirs. They seemed to die, but they really lived. What Herod meant for evil, God meant for good. Herod delivered them to heaven, peace, and joy without measure. They praised God, not by speaking but by dying. Their lives were emptied of themselves and filled with Him. They had no complaint. It was their mothers who were the victims.

This, then, is also your life in Christ. You are the victim, still suffering, still in sadness. Yet the life Christ lived, He lived for you in order to make Himself a sacrifice of redemption and atonement. The death He died, He died for you. And the resurrection to which He rose, He rose for you. And that suffering, dying, and rising now lives in you. Do not mourn, do not live, do not sleep, do not eat, do not move as those who have no hope. You have hope! Jesus lives. The kingdom of God is within you. He breaks you, empties you, dies in you, that He might rebuild, refill, and resurrect you. He calls you again out of Egypt. He calls you away from Pharoah's slavery to sin and death. He shows you the way of the cross and the way of life. If He makes you weak like a child, then in Him—only in Him, and always in Him—you are strong. Cast your burdens upon Him. He knows your pain. He loves you. Let go of your anger and jealousy. You are only hurting yourself. The Lord forgives you and desires to bring you home.

The boys of Bethlehem were not abandoned. You won't be either. There is hope in your future. Jesus loves you.

In ✠ Jesus' name. Amen.

St. Nicholas of Myra,
Bishop and Confessor

December 6

Hebrews 13:7-17
St. Matthew 25:14-23†

In the name of the Father and of the ✠ *Son and of the Holy Spirit. Amen.*

S t. Nicholas was the fearless bishop of Myra, a Greek city, in what is today Turkey. He was a courageous confessor who stood toe to toe with the emperor more than once and risked his life by calling him to repentance, for which he was imprisoned. He is also given credit as one of the authors of what we call the Nicene Creed. Legend says that he lost his temper at the council and slapped Arius, who was denying the divinity of Jesus Christ. He was zealous for the truth and intolerant of error.

The legend about the slapping is significant. The legend says that Nicholas' fellow bishops removed him from office for the offense. Christians do not respond in faith to heresy with violence. That is what Muslims do, not Christians. Nicholas thus repented the next day. He fell prey to the temptation of Satan and turned something good, zeal for the truth, into something evil. In accordance with the very character of grace, in response to his repentance, he was restored to the bishopric.

Today he is most famous for his charity and selfless giving. There are more legends about his anonymously helping the poor than any other topic, and, of course, much of his story has been corrupted into a shallow imitation of charity in the form of Santa Claus. For what it is worth, whatever he did, he did not bring mountains of toys to well-fed

---

† Common of a Confessor-Bishop from *Daily Divine Service Book*

children, warm and snug in their beds. If he was as charitable as the legends say, he was charitable to the poor.

The actual St. Nicholas, in his zeal for Christ and his love for the poor, is an inspiration for us. We rightly seek to imitate his faith and his good works. But especially in our culture we need to keep in mind which comes first. We expect that the legends are at least mostly true and that he was a generous and giving man. This should not be downplayed or dismissed. It is commendable. But for Nicholas the source of his charity was the point. He didn't plot to do good works. He was loved by Christ and was, in the first place, himself the recipient of charity, of generosity, of grace. He wasn't a man without sins or weaknesses; he was a man forgiven who lived in the joy of grace. That joy caused him to move out in love and mercy.

We should not be surprised that a man so zealous for the truth would also be zealous in works of mercy. The zeal is the same. It has the same source. And we should note that St. Nicholas is commemorated in the Church for being a bishop and confessor because the greatest charity is the release of men from the bonds of sin by the proclamation of Jesus Christ.

As a bishop, a man placed into the apostolic office by Christ, St. Nicholas ruled over us and spoke the word of God to us. We follow his faith and consider the outcome of his conduct. He is a not merely a teacher of the faith who has handed us the Creed but also a role model, even if his passions sometimes got the best of him.

And is the Creed which he has left us any different than the parable of the talents told by our Lord? Our Lord Jesus Christ, for us men and for our salvation, came down from heaven and was incarnate by the Holy Spirit of the Virgin Mary and was made man. This was so that He would be crucified for us under Pontius Pilate, that He might bestow gifts upon those who do not deserve them. That is the point of the parable. The Lord gives His kingdom away. He is not a harsh man. He does not reap where He does not sow. Rather, quite the opposite: He sows, that others who did not work might reap for free.

Who deserves this kingdom? No one. It is impossible to deserve a kingdom. But to you who have been given much in Holy Baptism and made His heirs, He gives even more. Your faith is multiplied like talents well-invested. It is you who, like St. Nicholas, reap where you did not sow, buy and eat without money, and never pay for your sins or debts. Jesus Christ, the Lord of Nicea, bestows upon you a kingdom which has no end.

In ✠ *Jesus' name. Amen.*

St. Lucy, Virgin and Martyr

December 13

2 Corinthians 10:17-11:2
St. Matthew 13:44-52

In the name of the Father and of the ✠ Son and of the Holy Spirit. Amen.

The kingdom of heaven is like the most wonderful, interesting, excellent, lovely thing that you can't imagine. It is beyond comprehension. It is impossible. It is like something that takes the place of every other thing, a treasure that is not sold but for which everything else is sold, a pearl that a merchant gives up his livelihood for—an impossibly perfect, wonderful, delightful thing.

That is what the kingdom of heaven is like. What the kingdom of heaven *is* is the reign of Christ our Lord in us, by the power of His death and resurrection. It is the grace of God, Christ Himself, living and reigning in you, His children. It is not a future event. It is a present reality.

Luther teaches us that when we pray in the Our Father "Thy kingdom come," it is not so much for the end of things as it is for His coming now. We pray that our heavenly Father would give us His Holy Spirit, *now*, so that by His grace we would believe and receive His holy Word, *now*, and lead godly lives, *now*, here in time and then there in eternity. The prayer includes a desire for the Lord's second coming, for His return on the last day, but it is mostly a desire and bid that He come and rule us now. Thus St. John the Baptist, that greatest of Advent preachers, preaches, "Repent, for the kingdom of heaven is at hand." It is not far away. It is near. It is now. It is, in fact, here at hand right now.

The death and resurrection of our Lord Jesus Christ, whereby He has made us His own and rules in us, is the only thing that actually matters or that makes anything else matter. It is greater than the greatest gifts of creation, without which no gift of creation has any joy. And it is now. If Christ had not redeemed the world, there would be no good things. It would be hell. Even those who do not believe in Him, who will not receive the eternal benefits of His grace, live now by grace and have the ability to find some joy in creation. But the only reason there is anything good in this fallen world is because it has been redeemed. Thus can we say, in that sense, that the redemption is the only thing that matters.

The redemption of creation—the rescue and payment for humanity, the love of God—is ridiculously and insanely great. It isn't economically sound. It is extravagant beyond imagination. The Creator and His grace, His undeserved love and kindness, comes for you now. He intervenes in history. He breaks into your life of His own accord. Uninvited, He comes, lifts you up, washes you off, and covers you with peace and joy.

This is the kingdom in which St. Lucy lived and died. The Emperor Diocletian could not hurt her with torture or execution. She was able to suffer it with marvelous dignity because she knew that it wasn't real. She knew that all the suffering and trappings of power, all the niceties and the poverty, all the droll day-in day-out struggles of a mundane peasant existence and the thrill of royal power are only a Satanic veneer, covering and hiding the reality of the Creator who is in control of His creation and actively involved, who promised St. Lucy in the waters of Holy Baptism that nothing ill would befall her, that her foot would not strike the stone.

She recognized Satan for what he is: a liar. She knew that he could neither deliver on the false promises he made nor carry out the false threats that he made. God Himself had rescued her from the fires of hell, made her His own. They tore out her eyes, but they could not touch her vision. She was forgiven, loved by God. Nothing could separate her from the bridegroom who gave His life for hers. So she stood before that evil magistrate and said, "Do your worst. You can harm me none. Only God can take my life. He is in control. He is good. I trust Him to be good to me."

So it is that God, in His mercy, at the right time, took her from this shadowy existence into the splendor of His light. He has made her passing an example of faith and her confession an inspiration for all of us still here.

But great as she is, she is not our queen; she is our sister. She has come to the reward laid up for her, but not for her alone. This, too, is your reward. The grace that found her in the despair of sin is the same grace that spoke you alive in the font of Jordan. You were baptized into Christ's baptism. You are anointed with Him for life, christened with His name and righteousness, joined in that one baptism to that one Lord in one faith, so also then to St. Lucy and all the saints.

Have you understood all these things? Yes, Lord. That is to say, we understand that they are true, that You are good and love us and are greater than anything in this world. We understand that this is beyond us and we believe it, even when reason, experience, and common sense fail us, even when it hurts or brings suffering. We submit to Your Word which never passes away. We believe that You are good and will be good to us, both now and then.

What joy is yours! The Lord Himself has commended you. The kingdom of heaven is here. It is in you.

In ✠ Jesus' name. Amen.

St. Thomas, Apostle

December 21

Judges 6:36-40
Ephesians 2:19-22
St. John 20:24-29

In the name of the Father and of the ✠ Son and of the Holy Spirit. Amen.

Just days before our commemoration of the swaddled babe's bed in the manger, the Church takes us to the Sunday after the resurrection, to St. Thomas' great confession. Here we see the destiny of the babe born to the Virgin, rejected by the innkeeper, scarred by the sins of selfish men, but alive by the power of the Most High. He is the Son of God and the Son of Mary, God in our skin, one of us but without the inherited corruption of Adam. As one of us He subjects Himself to the miseries of man, to the sufferings caused by sinners in a chaotic dog-eat-dog world. As an infant He will be swaddled with our sin. He will know hardship, hunger, loneliness, sorrow, and pain. He will suffer eternal damnation, lonely exile away from God, and torture in everlasting flames. In love He will rise and come through doors shut in fear to open Thomas' heart.

He was born to die our death. God raised up a sacrifice worthy of the great shame and scandal of our rebellion in Himself. He escaped Herod's wrathful rage and walked miraculously through crowds intent on killing Him. He was the appointed sacrifice, but in His own time and place. No one takes the life of the one whom the angels serve, but the Son of Man lays down His own life on His own accord, and He takes it up again. He is the ram in the thicket who takes our place, who dies in Isaac's bonded death, and in ours. The knife is seized by the holy angel at the last instant. Its downward thrust turned to the innocent victim. Justice is met. The ransom paid. The lamb dies. Isaac goes free.

The angel turned the knife on Him. He who knew no sin was swaddled in our sin to die our death, to be buried in the virgin tomb prepared for another man. The blood that issues from His wounds washes over us who should have died. It marks us and cleanses us. The angel of death passes over us to kill Him, and we are safe.

And yet this Son of Mary has no beginning and no ending. He is Alpha and Omega. He is outside of time. He is the light, the life, and the way. He became man and is still a man. As a man He died. As a man He rose. He is also God, Creator, Giver, Sustainer, Redeemer, and Savior. He is stronger than the strong one whom He defeated. Death cannot hold Him. He rested that last, great, and final Sabbath. Then He rose. His humiliation, His denial of His divine rights and powers as a man, is no more. He is exalted. As a man, as our brother, our distant kinsman, He now always and fully uses all that is His as God. He ascended to heaven and as our high priest rules at the right hand of His Father. Thomas sees Him, exalted, in the upper, fearful room. And by the grace of God working in the Holy Spirit, Thomas believes and confesses: "My Lord and my God."

At the command of Him who orders wind and wave, Thomas places his doubting hand into the side from whence flowed the water and the blood. He retracts his hand—now cleansed, now pure, now believing—like unto Moses removing his leprous hand cleansed from his breast. With God all things are possible. Thomas, the doubter, is ordained an apostle. He is sent to preach and he preaches to those who have not seen, and by that preaching they are blessed, that is, they hear the Word of God and believe. He lays that once-doubting hand, which felt the life-giving scars of God in the flesh, upon the sick, the dying, and those to be placed into his office, and they too are blessed. Having not seen but hearing the Word of God, they believe. They believe that the Word is flesh by way of the Virgin, was crucified and raised. They confess with Thomas that this Son of Mary is the God of Moses, the Lord, the great I AM who makes for Himself a people by grace. He is steadfast and compassionate. He did not give up on Thomas. He does not give us on us.

Thanks be to God for St. Thomas. His doubting has served our faith more than the belief of the other apostles. His physical touch has confirmed for us what the prophets have taught. Thus do we go, by faith, with leprous hands and hearts to be touched by Jesus in His Holy Communion. Here is the blood that issued from that pierced side, which cleanses our hearts and drives off doubt. Here is the body swaddled and laid in the animals' feeding trough, that we might eat better than kings. And that, dear friends, makes for a most piously merry and joyful Christmas.

In ✠ Jesus' name. Amen.

THE CONFESSION OF ST. PETER

January 18

Acts 4:8-13
2 Peter 1:1-15
St. Matthew 16:13-20

In the name of the Father and of the ✠ Son and of the Holy Spirit. Amen.

It is what men say that reveals who they are. None of us has the ability to conceal what is in his heart. It always comes out in the end on the tips of our tongues. That is why we try to cover up so much. That is why spin doctors exist. No politician has yet been born who could keep his mouth shut. How many times have you pretended that you forgot something that you hadn't? How many times have you pretended that you didn't mean what you said, when you did? How many times have you feigned shock and hurt because you had been misinterpreted, when you hadn't? It is what comes out of the mouth that defiles a man. The mouth reveals the heart.

Now if you cannot tell the truth about the simplest things; if you always color the facts, exaggerate, and edit; if you tell other people's stories as though they were your own; if you act like you are better than you are; if all this causes you to feel deep down inside like a phony, it is because your heart is black with sin and your mouth has shown it. Repent.

But notice this: Our Lord did not ask St. Peter what he was doing, whether his life was in order, whether he was improving the world, whether he was trying hard and making a difference, or whether he was honest. The kingdom of God is not built upon the good works of men. Nor did our Lord ask Peter what he believed, if he was rational or consistent, if his theology was accurate. The kingdom of God is not built upon faith.

Our Lord asked Peter, "Who do you say that I am?" Peter's answer was not his own. Flesh and blood did not reveal it to him. The Spirit who once hovered over the primordial chaotic waters of the universe, who lit upon the Messiah in the form of a dove, opened Peter's lips. Out came the Word of God: "You are the Christ, the Son of the living God." Upon this—the Word of God, the revelation of His love in the Messiah, on the lips of men—Christ builds His Church.

This is the way God builds. What Peter could not say, God said for him. God purified Peter from the inside out. He entered into Peter through his ear. And even though Peter was a sinner, sometimes a blow-hard, angry man and at other times a pietist who tried to force his dietary laws upon freed men, God still loved and used him. He entered into him by speaking the kingdom, and that kingdom in Peter opened Peter's lips. His lips were cleansed for confession. His mouth, by grace, declared God's praise: "You are the Christ, the Son of the living God." That is the way God builds. He is the actor, the architect, and the mason. He even provides the material. He does for Peter what Peter could not do for himself. He gives Peter His Word.

This is how He works also in you. Do not forget that for all your sin, you are baptized and have heard His Word. The Father has declared you well-pleasing to Him. The Spirit Himself has lit upon you. The Son has made you His home. You make confession like Peter before you. You sing God's praise, the profound reality that God has intervened in your life through grace. He has forgiven you for Jesus' sake. You are His own. You are holy, righteous, and innocent. You are free from making up your own songs, your own confessions, your own worship. You are free from making up your own questions and answers. God has built you into His Church through His Word upon the lips of men.

By His grace we can say a lot of things about who Jesus Christ is. He is the prophet greater than Moses. He is our redeemer, our shepherd king. He is the mercy seat, the grace-filled cloud that leads us out of slavery. He is the ram caught in the thicket who dies in our place. He is the suffering servant with pierced hands and feet, surrounded by the bulls of Bashan. He is the victor over death and the grave, who beckons us to come and eat and drink what we did not plant or earn, without cost and without money. He is the remover of Babel's curse, restoring us again to the brotherhood of humanity in the bond of the Spirit, with a single language of prayer. He removes the false divisions of color, ethnicity, and sex. He removes the distinctions of age and culture. He makes us one holy Christian Church and has revealed Himself to us in the Scriptures of the prophets.

What St. Peter says by inspiration is not new, nor does it belong to him alone. "You are the Christ, the Son of the living God" embodies all of the Old Testament, all of our hope and faith, all that we are in Christ. It is God's confession, and He gives it to you as well as to Peter. It rises up from your heart, made pure by grace, through lips cleansed in Holy Baptism and Holy Communion. It is your confession. Jesus is the Christ, the Son of the living God. You are Petros, a rock of Jesus Christ, and the gates of hell will not overcome you.

In ✠ Jesus' name. Amen.

Commemoration of Sarah, Holy Woman

January 19

1 Timothy 5:3-10
St. Matthew 13:44-52

In the name of the Father and of the ✠ Son and of the Holy Spirit. Amen.

Before we can talk about the parables at hand or Sarah, we need to talk about parables. The incarnation of our Lord Jesus Christ has so tied Him to our cause and so intimately tied us to the Godhead that it can, in fact, be difficult to tell the difference between the Christian and the Christ when reading the Scriptures.

Consider these words of our Lord:

> Then the disciples came and said to him, "Why do you speak to them in parables?" And he answered them, "To you it has been given to know the secrets of the kingdom of heaven, but to them it has not been given. For to the one who has, more will be given, and he will have an abundance, but from the one who has not, even what he has will be taken away. This is why I speak to them in parables, because seeing they do not see, and hearing they do not hear, nor do they understand. Indeed, in their case the prophecy of Isaiah is fulfilled that says:

> 'You will indeed hear but never understand,
>   and you will indeed see but never perceive.'
> For this people's heart has grown dull,
>   and with their ears they can barely hear,
> and their eyes they have closed,
>   lest they should see with their eyes
> and hear with their ears

and understand with their heart
and turn, and I would heal them.

But blessed are your eyes, for they see, and your ears, for
they hear. For truly, I say to you, many prophets and
righteous people longed to see what you see, and did not
see it, and to hear what you hear, and did not hear it."
(Matt. 13:10-17)

The parables of our Lord, in particular, are best understood as
revealing something to us of His character and mission. They are never
meant to reveal how God is like us but rather how God is unlike us.
Still, the Christ is an example for us. He has demonstrated what it is
to perfectly trust in God, and we go too far if we do not see something
of ourselves, as Christians, in the parables as well as seeing who He is.

For example, we should see that the Good Samaritan is, above all,
a Christ figure. It is Christ who rescues those who were left half-dead
by the Law, who binds up their wounds, who pays for everything, and
who promises to come back. It is the Christ who is the despised outsider,
moved by compassion, to love His neighbor. And yet we should not
neglect the example of mercy nor the explicit call to go and do likewise.
The Good Samaritan is chiefly Christ. He is the metaphoric answer to
the lawyer's question and not a call to good works or a damning of
the man to hell, which the Law had already accomplished. But insofar
as Christ is an example for us and is the most perfect Christian, the
Samaritan is also a demonstration of how mercy is lived out.

The Christian rightly identifies himself with Christ. So he should
see himself with, and model himself on, the Samaritan. After all, when
our Lord instructs us to pick up our cross and follow Him, He is not
telling us to die for the sins of the world, or even that we should work off
our own sins by sacrifice, but He is telling us to live and die like He did.

This is not to say that the parables have multiple meanings. Rather,
the parables reveal something of the divine character of the Messiah

and His radical love for us. He is not like us, but we should be like Him. Creation echoes and mirrors its Creator. His fingerprints are upon us. That is true even of the unregenerate, but it is more true of those who have been recreated and reborn. So it is not multiple meanings but rather limitless applications and things to ponder.

The first two parables today are best understood as Christ Himself acting. The kingdom is like a man who finds a treasure, hides it, and then sells all that he has to have it. That field is the world's graveyard. The buried treasure is the sons and daughters of Adam who have returned to dust. The Lord sells all that He has to dig them up and revive them. They are worth everything to Him. The sons and daughters of Adam can also be likened to a pearl of great price, that for which the Lord sought eagerly and across the ends of the earth since the Fall, and it is worth all that He has.

But so also is the Christ worth everything to the Christian. Christ is found without cost, like a treasure hidden in a field, unexpected and undeserved, but open and available and accessible to all. And yet, at the same time, to possess this treasure is not without price, for heavenly riches are not obtained without the loss of this world. Indeed, the cost is nothing compared to the gift. To obtain the gift is only to give up sin, gossip, hatred, and lust; it is to give up nothing, but it is a cost. Or else we might think of the cost as being removed from this world and hated by this world, losing this world and gaining the devil as an enemy.

This brings us to the third parable. This parable discloses something of the dark side of the Gospel. All are paid for and all are loved, but not all receive the benefit. There is a place of weeping and gnashing of teeth. Some sons of Adam would climb back into the coffin. Some of them would not give up hangovers and venereal diseases and embarrassment; they cling to the flesh and this world and to their father, the devil, with all their might. Not only do they despise the one who rescued them, but they cannot see themselves as a treasure or a pearl. They insist on being Satan's playthings, and they are thrown into the fiery furnace by choice.

"Have you understood all these things?" asks our Lord. The disciples said yes. Sarah probably would have snorted in laughter.

The disciples did not understand, but they were not rebuked. We might hear their answer as arrogance, but it wasn't. It was zeal. They were filled with the Holy Spirit. They knew not what they were saying, but they were sincere, not unlike the confirmands whom we ask to pledge such great things. The Lord does not mock them or rebuke them. He simply states the glory of their office. They are His children. They understand in part. They receive His Word and they believe it. And they will bring out of the Lord's treasure what is new and what is old. They will bring out delightful things, treasures and pearls, and they will uncover in the sons and daughters of Adam pearls and treasures for the Lord. For the Lord's people are His pearls and treasures.

What has this to do with Sarah? Well, she mocked the Lord's promise. Then she denied it. Her life had been hard, to be sure. She was old and she was barren and she was frustrated. She had made a grave error in handing over Hagar to her husband, and twice her husband had tried to hand her over to other men. So we can certainly understand her snorted disbelief at the Lord's promise of a son. But that was a sin, a mocking of God, and when she was asked about it she denied it because she was afraid of God's wrath. God's response to her denial is surprising. It was simply, "Yes, you did," and that was it. He turned her niece into a pillar of salt for the very human-seeming reaction of turning around to look at the city she was leaving, but Sarah gets nothing more than a mild correction: "Yes, you did."

The Holy Spirit in Hebrews tells us that Sarah conceived Isaac by faith. She counted the Lord as faithful, despite the terrible things she had suffered, the long years she had waited, and her initial surprise and denial. Finally, she was given a son. And what does she say then? She says, "God has made laughter for me; everyone who hears will laugh with me."

Once she laughed in derision. Now she laughs with joy and God laughs with her. She is unashamed to be an old lady with a baby. The Lord replaced her mockery and cynicism with joy. It is not simply that the Lord is gentle, and He certainly doesn't wink at our sins. Rather, it is this: the Lord loved Sarah more than Abraham did. He counted her as a treasure and wouldn't let go of her even when she tried to let go of Him. That love caused her to repent and believe, and it brought laughter into her house.

And through that laughter came the Messiah who paid for all her sins and for all of ours. The kingdom of heaven is like a cynical, barren, old woman restored to her husband, given a child, and filled with joy. That is what it has to do with Sarah.

In ✠ Jesus' name. Amen.

St. Timothy,
Confessor, Bishop, and Martyr

January 24

Acts 16:1-5
1 Timothy 6:11-16
St. Matthew 24:42-47

In the name of the Father and of the ✠ Son and of the Holy Spirit. Amen.

St. Paul left Timothy in Ephesus to be the pastor. It was not the nicest thing Paul ever did. Undoubtedly, Timothy would have preferred to continue in Paul's retinue. Then, having left him in the thick of things, he tells him to fight the good fight of the faith.

Faith is a fight. It is a fight against the flesh. You must flee the old man that clings to you. You must fight him all the way to the grave or to the Lord's return in glory. Faith is a fight also against the devil and his demons. It is resistance against the popular and convenient lies that they tell to lead men away from God. It is a stubborn refusal to be led by your eyes or by reason. It is a militant loyalty to the Word of God, the voice of the Shepherd. Faith is always a fight. There is no rest from it on this side of glory. The Church Militant is the Church at war, the Church fighting, and no one gets out of it alive.

It is considered a scandal that our war is waged primarily within our own ranks, within the Church. Bureaucrats obsessed with public image and terrified of decline can't understand it. "I thought they would know us by our love," they say. "Why don't we seem very loving? We need more honey to attract the flies. You people who are fighting all the time, fussing about doctrine, are ruining everything. Jesus wants us to be effective. Shape up, people. Stop fighting already."

But as it is inside each believer, so it is in the Church. The fight of the faith is fought primarily against oneself, on the inside. St. Paul was an accomplice to murder. Moses did the deed himself. We all harbor hate and lust and envy in our hearts. We all betray the Lord in our flesh and are guilty of murder, adultery, and idolatry. Our problem is not that we fought, but that we haven't fought as hard as we should have or we have fought for the wrong things.

The surprising thing is that it is from sinners that God makes sheep and saints. He drags them through. It is hard. It is tiring. Ever present is the temptation to sloth. That doesn't mean simply to be lazy, as it is often understood, but more precisely to be slothful is to give up the fight, to give up hope, to quit and give in. That is why it is one of the seven deadly sins. It is far worse than being lazy. It is quitting. The devil whispers in our ears, "Why can't we all just get along? Let's not be so picky. Let's have peace here, peace now, peace from this troublesome doctrine that divides men. Let's have some growth, some success, some honor in this world, some feeling of accomplishment." And it is tempting, to be sure. The predator knows his prey. He knows how weary we've become, how no one seems to really notice or care when we resist temptation, how we seem to get away with sin, how much we'd like to be popular and rich and win.

Thus did Paul warn Timothy: "Fight the good fight of the faith. Take hold of the eternal life to which you were called. Remember who you are. These baubles of the devil never satisfy. He has burned you before. He cannot be trusted. But the Word of God never fails, never changes, never lies. Jesus is the Son in whom the Father is well pleased. Listen to Him."

The Lord is ever faithful and patient. He justifies the believer. He declares His righteousness to be yours. He forgives sins, strengthens faith, and comforts with the peace that passes all understanding. And He does this to sinners, to fighters, to imperfect and selfish people. He cleanses the hearts of men by drowning the old man and raising up again a new man in His image. God our Savior desires all men to be saved and to come to the knowledge of the truth, for there is one God and one mediator between God and men: the man Christ Jesus, who gave Himself a ransom for all, to be testified in due time.

He will not abandon or forsake you. He has won the war. He will keep His promise. He will win the fight in you.

In ✠ Jesus' name. Amen.

The Conversion of St. Paul

January 25

Acts 9:1-22
St. Matthew 19:27-30

In the name of the Father and of the ✠ Son and of the Holy Spirit. Amen.

All over the world today, logophiles will be gathering to toast the Scottish Bard.† In most places, they will read these famous lines from the poem "To A Mouse":

> But Mousie, thou art no thy-lane,
> In proving foresight may be vain:
> The best laid schemes o' Mice an' Men
> > Gang aft agley,
> An' lea'e us nought but grief an' pain,
> > For promis'd joy!

Translated, it means that the mouse is not alone. The ability to build houses where men do not plow is no guarantee that the houses will not be destroyed. The best-laid schemes of mice and men go awry and leave us nothing but grief and pain where they promised joy.

Burns goes on:

> Still, thou art blest, compar'd wi' me!
> The present only toucheth thee:
> But Och! I backward cast my e'e.
> > On prospects drear!
> An' forward, tho' I canna see,
> > I guess an' fear!‡

---

† A Burns supper is an event held on January 25ᵗʰ, the birthday of Scottish poet Robert Burns, which recognizes his life and poetry.

‡ Robert Crawford and Christopher MacLachlan, eds., *The Best Laid Schemes: Se-*

The mouse is blessed, in Burns' mind, because she is free of a conscience that knows regret and sorrow. It is shallow, in a sense, but being free from memory and experience, she can face the future without fear.

My fellow earth-born companions, mortal men, why was Burns afraid? What so haunted him that he would count a mouse, newly evicted from her winter home, with no grass or stubble at hand, as more blessed than he? The mouse was startled at his plow, but Burns was the truly timid beast, full of sadness and regret, for he thought that God must remain unknown. He thought that no plans could be so well laid that they would not go awry and end in grief and pain.

Perhaps Burns would have been correct if it were not that Jesus Christ became a man and laid a plan so well that it has endured these thousands of years and will never, never end. More blessed than a mouse or an honest man or a working dog is the man who knows Jesus Christ as Lord, who sees upon Zion's cruel scaffolds a God who plans well to rescue man, to make atonement for all his wrongs, to pronounce peace and good will for them by divine and perfect love. He prepares a place for them where plows do not turn up and destroy. This love is far greater than a red, red rose, newly sprung in June. The sea will go dry. The rocks will melt with the sun. But it is no vanity or boast, no havering, to say that this love will endure forever. This love will move men from the place where plans of mice and men run awry to the place where God's perfect grace orders all things, where mice and men, lambs and wolves lie down together without regrets or fears or animosity.

Thus it was for St. Paul, that one-time hater of God. He laid his plans for Damascus, but by God's grace they went awry. He was recruited from the darkness to the light. He changed sides. He found that his pursuer was not a killing, angry God, tearing up the earth with a vengeful plow, but the bleeding, providing, nurturing Savior who only wanted to forgive and love him. Paul was baptized! A miracle occurred.

lected Poetry and Prose of Robert Burns (Princeton: Princeton University Press, 2009), 48.

Paul, one-time killer of the elect, believed that Jesus was the Christ and that even he could be forgiven and loved by God. He found the peace that passes all understanding, peace for which Burns longed but which Burns sadly refused. So it was that St. Paul was prepared to face death in a Roman jail without fear or regret, for he knew that the God known in Jesus Christ would ever be good to him, even give him a throne and a crown, and would not leave him destitute or alone.

Herein lies the chief difference between Burns and Paul: Paul had hope. May God, in His mercy, plant the same in us.

In ✠ Jesus' name. Amen.

SCRIPTURE INDEX

Old Testament

New Testament